Mountain Biking Santa Cruz

The Ultimate Trail & Ride Guide for the Santa Cruz Area

2nd Edition

Dave & Allison Diller

EXTREMELINE™
PRODUCTIONS LLC

2009

© 2009 Extremeline Productions LLC

ISBN-10 0-9723361-2-5
ISBN-13 978-0-9723361-2-3

2nd Edition
Printed in the USA

All photos, graphs, and maps by the authors; ©2009
Cover: Zane Gray Trail; Above Photo: Aptos Rancho Trail

www.**EXTREMELINE**.com
EXTREMELINE PRODUCTIONS LLC
BOOKS@EXTREMELINE.COM
PO BOX 1194 KERNVILLE, CA 93238

Please Read This Important Information Before Using This Book!

Beware! Mountain biking is a high-risk activity! Could it be fun any other way? This book is a general guide that does not reveal all of the possible dangers associated with the described trails or the hazards of riding. Neither is it a substitute for common sense, discretion, good judgement, and personal responsibility. If you lack these, stay on your couch and don't even consider getting on a bike!

If you are not confident in your ability to ride, detect trail conditions and obstacles, properly maintain your bike, read signs, keep a sense of direction, and adapt to changing conditions; don't rely on this book! Instead, get a GPS with all relevant topo-maps, satellite photos, an official forest ranger guide, a bike coach, a survival kit, full body armor, and very carefully walk and inspect all trails before riding them.

The level of difficulty ratings and descriptions in this book are completely subjective and relative to other rides in the area. Although based on GPS-mapping technology, the depicted maps, mileages, and descriptions are only to be used as an aid and may not reflect the real world. The trails and trail conditions can change on a daily basis due to weather, types of users, and numerous other factors.

Each biker and reader of this book is the master of his/her own destiny, and has the choice to obey signs, only ride legal trails, wear proper protective gear, and check the current conditions and trail-use policy before riding.

The publisher and authors are not responsible or liable for any inaccuracies, errors and omissions, changes in policy, trail closures or re-routes, trail conditions and changes, or for any injuries, deaths, accidents, suffering, losses, and other relevant (or irrelevant) factors.

By opening or utilizing this book in any way, the reader and/or biker acknowledges the above statements and agrees to expressly assume any and all risk of injury or death associated with the use of this book; and to indemnify, not to sue, and release from all liability Extremeline Productions LLC, the authors, members, managers, and all associated people involved with this book.

Table of Contents

Autumn singletrack at Saratoga Gap.

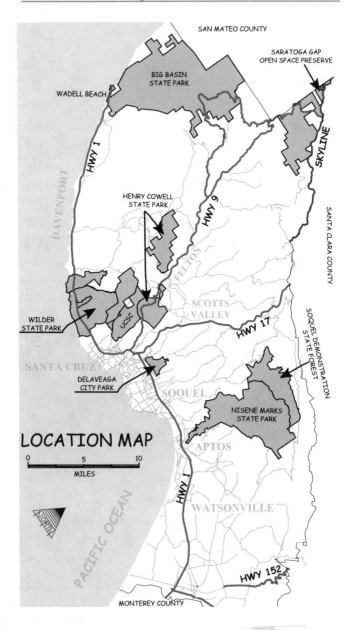

Welcome to Santa Cruz

Encompassed by the Pacific Ocean and vast amounts of public land, this coastal mecca of mountain biking has year round riding with a variety of enticing trails and gorgeous scenery.

Containing more state parks than any other county, Santa Cruz offers one of the most diverse and beautiful coastal environments on the planet. From the surf to the mountains, you can bike a myriad of trails: along pristine creeks in a shady redwood forest, through sunny grasslands, or on the scenic coastal cliffs. An abundance of wildlife will often add an exhilarating surprise to anyone's ride.

An evening out in Santa Cruz.

Get ready to ride roller coaster singletrack, bomb fast and furious fire roads, test your skills on technical trails, or simply cruise the many rides. There are plenty of options for all ability levels whether you want a scenic family ride or a gnarly downhill technical challenge. It is no wonder that Bike Magazine has declared Santa Cruz both a "mecca," and a "mountain biking paradise" with "incredible trails."

Mountain biking in Santa Cruz will not only thrill you, it will make you stoked on life! Completely immersed in nature, you'll glide through an ancient giant redwood grove then charge toward the massive surf as you bike down the coastal mountains. Mountain biking here is an incredible experience!

About This Guidebook

The Book

This pocket-sized guide is meant to be as transportable and versatile as a mountain biker. While providing specific information about mountain biking in Santa Cruz, it will aid you in choosing and locating appropriate trails and rides.

The book is divided into sections based on state parks or specific riding areas. In each section, an introduction is given and the particular rides of the area are depicted. Trail details and directions are provided for each ride along with accurate maps and elevation profiles created with the latest GPS mapping technology. In addition, a "Trail Guide" section, which compares and details specific trails, is provided for many of the state parks that have a myriad of riding choices. These elements will enable you, the biker, to have the freedom and ability to piece together your own perfect biking adventure.

Ratings and Ride Details

Location: General area of the ride.

Distance: Measured in miles.

Elevation: Depicts the minimum and maximum elevation you will encounter on the ride.

Trail Surface: Explains what kind of trail you'll be riding.

Type of Ride: Defines the ride either as a Loop, Out & Back, or One-Way.

Terrain: Tells you about the surrounding environment and scenery of the ride.

Technical Level: Describes how difficult the trail is to bike, relative to other Santa Cruz trails.

<u>Easy</u>: Usually fairly smooth dirt road or wide trail.

<u>Medium</u>: Some roots, ruts, rocks, and/or potholes with some maneuvering involved; often on a tighter trail.

<u>Difficult</u>: Narrow trail with bigger tree roots, ruts, small drop-offs, and/or rocks scattered about; some steep sections.

<u>Most Difficult</u>: Steep and rough, large obstacles, frequent changes in gradient; hike-a-bike likely in some sections.

Exertion Level: The general aerobic level of a ride.

<u>Mild:</u> Generally, the ride is flat with little or no climbing.

<u>Moderate</u>: Hills with some gradual or short steep climbs.

<u>Strenuous</u>: Longer and steeper uphill sections that could potentially cause excessive panting and sweating.

<u>Very Strenuous</u>: Heart pounding, mega uphill sections.

Highlights: A brief description of the main features of the ride to get you pumped up!

Options: Ways to lengthen, shorten, or add variety to the ride.

Note: Anything deserving attention about the ride.

Directions/Access: Driving (or biking) directions to the trailhead. When mileage is given from Santa Cruz, it refers specifically to the intersection of Highway 17 and Highway 1 ("The Fishhook") unless otherwise specified.

Ride Profile: This graph depicts the ride in terms of elevation gain and loss related to mileage - so you know what to expect. The major changes in elevation and key features are shown. Please keep in mind that the scope of the profiles may require that quick changes in elevation be left out. Because of the variety in the elevation and the length of different rides depicted, exact comparisons between profiles can not be made without taking these factors into account.

Mileage Guide: Provides key features and a description of the ride, which will hopefully prevent you from getting lost. They are labeled in miles for those with either bike computers or mathematically gifted minds. Mileages will vary among individual GPS and bike computers.

Map Legend

– – – – – – – – –	SINGLETRACK
· · · · · · · · · · ·	NO BIKES TRAIL
═ ═ ═ ═ ═ ═ ═	FIRE ROAD
═ ═ ═ ═ ═ ═ ═	GRADED DIRT ROAD
———————	PAVED ROAD
———————	MAIN PAVED ROAD
▬▬▬▬▬▬▬	HIGHWAY
++++++++++++++++++	TRAIN TRACKS
– ·· – ·· – ·· – ·· –	PROPERTY BOUNDARY
———————	RIVER OR CREEK

▲	NORTH ARROW	↙	RIDE DIRECTION
Ⓟ	RIDE PARKING	△	CAMPING AREA
ⓟ	OTHER PARKING	▪■	BUILDINGS
★	RIDE START	🏠	RESTROOM
⅞	PICNIC AREA	•—	GATE

Index of Rides by Category

Use this short index as a basic reference tool to select what kind of ride you prefer; whether it be Sweet Singletrack, Mellow Cruisers, Technical Tests, Hardcore Climbs, Insane Downhills, Expedition Big-Day Rides, Multi-Interest Rides, Quick Fixes, Multi-Park/Interregional Rides, or Santa Cruz Classics. (Page 180).

Santa Cruz Climate

Santa Cruz offers good year round riding conditions. While the overall climate is mild, occasionally it will be significantly colder and rainier in winter. Summer is not always hot either; cold fog and breezes near the coast can make it quite chilly. At the same time, the inland areas may be very hot and "Indian summers" can warm the whole coastal region late in the year. If you are unsure of the weather, it is best to be prepared for any situation by wearing layers.

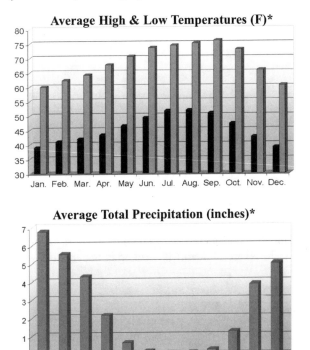

Average High & Low Temperatures (F)*

Average Total Precipitation (inches)*

Period of Record: 7/1/1948 to 12/31/2000; Data from Western Regional Climate Center; www.rcc.dri.edu

Monthly Sunset Times (standard time)**

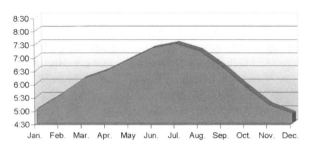

Monthly Sunrise Times (standard time)**

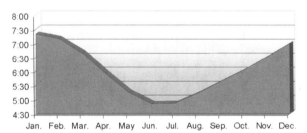

**Times are in Standard Time. Add 1 hour for Day Light Savings Time (DST).

Other Considerations

The following considerations are nothing to stress about, but it helps to be aware of them while riding in Santa Cruz.

Poison Oak

Beware! Santa Cruz has an abundance of poison oak, particularly near creeks and moist forested areas. Try to avoid crashing in it as you mountain bike around Santa Cruz! This stuff will have you scratching like a dog.

Stinging Nettles

Like poison oak, these plants are also abundant near creeks. Instantly you'll know what they are if you brush up against this plant. Don't worry: the sting goes away!

Ticks

Watch out for these annoying little pests in the brush, especially in early Spring. Its wise to check yourself periodically, especially if you find yourself bailing out in the bushes!

Mountain Lions

Mountain lions have been reported in all of the local parks, although it is very rare to see one. Consider yourself privileged if you spot one! However, it is obviously important to be extremely cautious around them.

Mountain Biking Ethics

 IMBA'S Trail Rules

Across the country thousands of miles of dirt trails have been closed to mountain bicyclists in recent years. The irresponsible riding habits of a few riders have been a factor. Do your part to maintain trail access by observing the following rules of the trail, formulated by IMBA (International Mountain Bicycling Association). Extensive mountain bike and trail access information can be found on their website: www.imba.com.

1. Ride on open trails only.
2. Leave no trace.
3. Control your bicycle.
4. Always yield trail.
5. Never spook animals.
6. Plan ahead.

 Author's Trail Law

Respect all of creation for your enjoyment and for all those who follow. Use common sense and keep mountain bike trails open by respecting the rules. Always be joyful, ride your best, and have lots of fun!

 Multi-Use Trails

Many of the trails around Santa Cruz are "multi-use", meaning that horses and hikers may appear at anytime. Please be cautious and alert when riding.

Lets keep trails open by always being considerate to all users.

Singletrack & Unauthorized Trails

Santa Cruz is often known for many of its unauthorized trails. Despite the fact that many of these trails are either on private property, for hiking only, or are closed for environmental and other reasons; they sometimes get ridden simply because they are great singletrack trails. However, riding unauthorized trails may hurt the overall mountain biking community by causing even more trail closures. (Or, maybe it will give the land managers a hint).

If you would like to see more singletrack opened to the public, become involved politically by contacting elected officials and joining a mountain bike advocacy group such as Mountain Bikers of Santa Cruz (MBOSC.org). As more mountain bikers voice their opinions, politicians and park officials will listen. While the authors would absolutely love to see more singletrack open to bikers, this book strongly encourages bikers to respect the laws and ride the many designated trails.

When non-biking or unauthorized trails are mentioned and/or shown on maps in this book, it is for the purpose of identifying your location in respect to the other trails that you may see in the area.

Enchanted Loop Trail on the wilder side of Wilder Ranch State Park.

Wilder Ranch State Park

Modern day fun on Old Cabin Trail.

If you've been yearning for one big bike park with dazzling terrain and mind-bending vistas close to town; Wilder Ranch is the bomb!

Whatever you desire; singletrack, fire roads, open meadows, forest, creeks, coastal terraces, valleys, ocean views, dirt, rocks, sand…its all just north of Santa Cruz waiting to be ridden! Containing almost 40 miles of multi-use trails throughout 6,000 acres, Wilder Ranch (including the addition of Gray Whale Ranch) is a mecca of California mountain biking.

Undoubtedly, all devout mountain biking pilgrims eventually find themselves ritually exploring this interwoven network of trails.

Views, singletrack, sun...welcome to Wilder Ranch.

Once a prospering dairy operation and a major practice spot for the rodeo circuit, Wilder Ranch is now active with a 22-acre historical ranch complex. This Cultural Preserve also provides evidence of Native American habitation and a Spanish mission adobe building. Cattle grazing and agriculture are still active in the area.

Wilder Ranch is located just a couple miles north of Santa Cruz off of Highway 1. The park is open for mountain biking between 8 am and sunset. Parking inside the State Park costs $6; annual passes are available. A great option is to ride the bike path from town (Ride 32). Dogs aren't allowed on trails.

Contemplate life before mountain bikes at the Cultural Preserve.

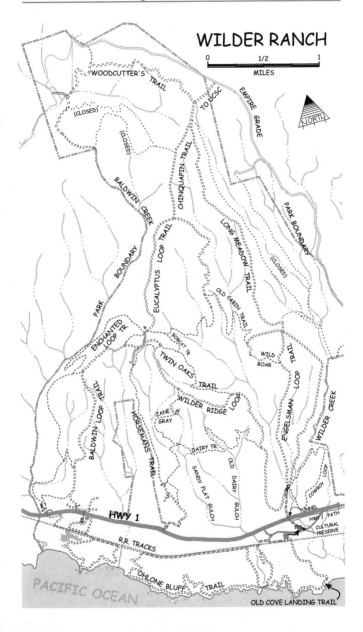

Old Cove Landing/Ohlone Bluff Trail

Its not tough to ride the bluffs.

Location: 2 miles past Western Dr. just north of Santa Cruz.

Distance: 1-14 miles roundtrip.

Elevation: 0/60 ft.

Trail Surface: 23% wide trail; 77% dirt road & doubletrack.

Type of Ride: Out & back.

Terrain: Ocean cliffs; grasslands; beaches; natural bridges, farm land.

Technical Level: Easy; an optional steep section involves descending a beach bluff, crossing a beach (which may be washed out), and climbing back up at Old Cove. You can also ride around the cove, rather than descend to the beach.

Exertion Level: Mild; almost completely flat.

Highlights: With the big backdrop of the massive Pacific Ocean, this incredibly beautiful ride meanders along miles of pristine California coastline. As you ride above several coves, deserted beaches, and rock outcroppings, keep your eyes open for wildlife. Seals, sea lions, dolphins, whales, birds, bobcats, and other wildlife often appear throughout the ride. Particularly awe-inspiring at sunset and when there are large waves, this is a "must-do" Santa Cruz ride for any level biker!

Options: Most people ride this as an out & back and simply turn around when they feel like it. A much longer ride is possible with the addition of the other inland Wilder Ranch trails, such as the Baldwin Loop Trail (Ride 3).

Note: Be prepared: since this ride is right on the ocean, it can occasionally be breezy and cool along the trail even in midsummer. Also, note that there are many farm roads on the inland side. At some points in the ride, the trail merges with these roads as you pass around the larger coves.

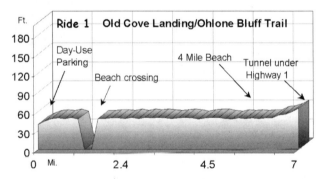

Directions/Access: In Santa Cruz, take Highway 1 North through town (Mission St). About 2 miles from the outskirts of town, turn left into Wilder Ranch State Park when you see the brown sign on the right. To enter the parking lot, pass through the entrance booth. The day-use parking will be on the right and costs $6. Alternative free parking is in the dirt pullouts out on Highway 1, but it's fairly inconvenient. Don't leave valuables in the car on Hwy 1! If you are riding from town, take the paved bike path that parallels Hwy 1 (see Ride 32).

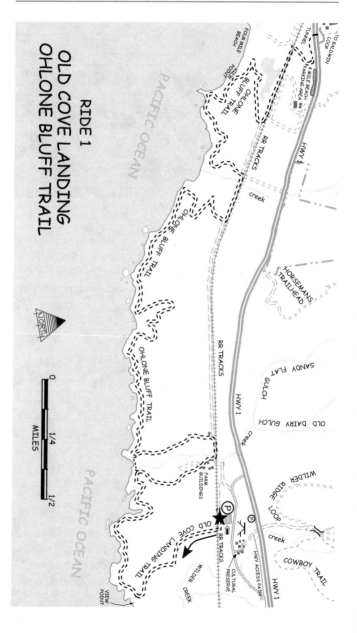

RIDE 1
OLD COVE LANDING
OHLONE BLUFF TRAIL

PACIFIC OCEAN

NORTH

0   1/4   1/2
MILES

PACIFIC OCEAN

OHLONE BLUFF TRAIL

OHLONE BLUFF TRAIL

OHLONE BLUFF TRAIL

FOUR MILE BEACH

BLUFF POINT

RR TRACKS

creek

RR TRACKS

RR TRACKS

TUNNEL

TO BALDWIN LOOP

4 MILE BEACH PARKING AREA

HWY 1

HORSEMAN'S TRAILHEAD

SANDY FLAT

GULCH

OLD DAIRY GULCH

WILDER

RIDGE

LOOP

COWBOY TRAIL

HWY 1

creek

HWY ACCESS PATH

CULTURAL PRESERVE

FARM BUILDINGS

P

OLD COVE LANDING TRAIL

WILDER CREEK

VIEW POINT

A rugged coastline embroidered with pristine beaches.

Mileage Guide	
0.0	From the information panel near the parking lot and restrooms, head toward the beach by taking the dirt trail just ahead. It is labeled "Old Cove Landing Trail." Soon, the trail merges left onto a dirt path and crosses train tracks.
.60	On the left, a viewing platform and information panel overlooks Wilder Beach. As the route skirts along the bluffs, keep your eyes open for natural bridges, ocean life, birds, bobcats, etc!
1.3	Keep pedaling along the cliffs as the trail merges with the dirt road around the cove.
1.6	As the road comes to a large cove, there are a couple options. Some riders take a steep trail that goes down the cliff to the beach, which is often inundated with water in the winter, and continues up the other side. This will put you at Mile 2.5 on this Mileage Guide. If the tide is too high and you want hassle-free biking, keep riding inland on the dirt road to get around the cove.
2.0	As you ride inland, you will enter a farm equipment area with a state park sign; go straight (passing a road on the left) and pedal through the area. Then turn left and ride along the train tracks for a short section. (Turning right leads to a shortcut back to the parking area via a dirt road on the inland side of the train tracks.)

2.2	From the tracks, veer left up a short hill. Just before you reach the shed, make a sharp left to head back toward the ocean on a narrow grassy doubletrack/path.
2.5	Soon you will be back on the cliffs! On the left, the beach trail merges. Continue rolling along the cliffs.
4.8	Just before the railroad tracks, go left and ride along side them.
5.1	Pedal left and head back toward the beach.
6.0	Peeks of 4-Mile Beach appear through the trees. From this scenic place, you'll often spot surfers shredding up the waves. Many people opt to ride back from this point. To keep riding to the beach or to the Baldwin Loop, continue on around the estuary as you pass agriculture fields.
6.5	As you reach the train tracks again (and an intersection of farm roads), turn left and ride along side.
6.7	4-way intersection with stop signs for crossing the tracks! Left goes down to 4-Mile Beach. To reach the tunnel under Highway 1 and the Baldwin Loop, go right and cross the tracks. Stay left on the path (a parallel road veers right) and come to an open intersection area. Go left on a beat-up asphalt road and look for the posted singletrack dropping on the left. Take this to the bike tunnel.
7.0	Bike tunnel under Hwy 1. Continuing on will take you up the Baldwin Loop Trail (Rides 3 and 6A). Otherwise turn around and head back. (Some people will also loop back on the railroad/farm roads.)

Scenic beauty can overwhelm any sense of direction.

Wilder Ridge Loop

Monterey Bay as seen from the Wilder Ridge Loop.

Location: Off of Highway 1, just north of Santa Cruz.

Distance: 8.2 miles.

Elevation: 25/630 ft.

Trail Surface: 46% singletrack; 54% fire road.

Type of Ride: Loop.

Terrain: Coastal grasslands; sparse forest; ridges, large vistas.

Technical Level: Medium/Difficult; some steep and bumpy sections.

Exertion Level: Moderate/Strenuous; lots of climbing at first but mostly gradual.

Highlights: Besides exhibiting stupendous views, this ride rates high on the fun factor! Most of the initial climbing is on a fire road exposed to nonstop panoramic ocean vistas, while rewarding singletrack completes most of the loop. The "Dairy Mill Trail" section grooves and winds its way in and out of gulleys, while the "Horseman's Trail" section will thrill those who love steep bumpy fast-paced frolics.

Options: Combine with other Wilder or Gray Whale Trails to lengthen the ride. Zane Gray Trail is also a popular singletrack option that bisects the loop for a shorter ride.

Note: Condition and quality of the trails vary seasonally.

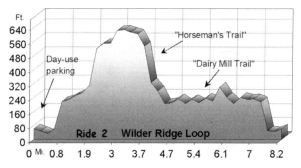

Directions/Access: See Directions/Access on Ride 1.

Mileage Guide	
0.0	From the Wilder Ranch day-use parking area, ride downhill on the paved road from the restrooms.
.15	Turn left at the Cultural Preserve and walk your bikes through this area to the bike tunnel ahead.
.40	At the split, after passing the information panel, ride left up Wilder Ridge Loop (signed on the left).
1.2	Continue climbing straight ahead (right) at the Wilder Ridge Loop split.
2.0	Split. Twin Oaks Trail veers right. This option can be taken if you prefer to climb singletrack (this will put you just above the Mile 3.2 turnoff on this Mileage Guide). Otherwise, grunt up this next steep section.
2.2	A welcome excuse to relieve lactic-acid-filled legs is located on the left; this viewpoint looks out upon much

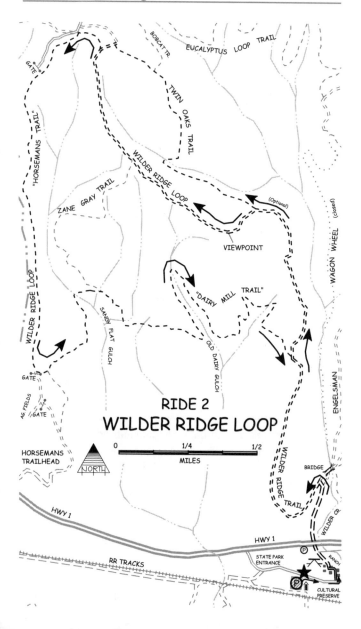

BOBCAT TR

EUCALYPTUS LOOP TRAIL

GATE

TWIN OAKS TRAIL

"HORSEMANS TRAIL"

WILDER RIDGE LOOP

ZANE GRAY TRAIL

(Optional)

VIEWPOINT

WAGON WHEEL (closed)

WILDER RIDGE LOOP

"DAIRY MILL TRAIL"

SANDY FLAT GULCH

OLD DAIRY GULCH

GATE

AG FIELDS

GATE

ENGELSMAN

**RIDE 2
WILDER RIDGE LOOP**

HORSEMANS TRAILHEAD

0   1/4   1/2

NORTH

MILES

WILDER RIDGE TRAIL

BRIDGE

WILDER CR

HWY 1

HWY 1

P

RR TRACKS

STATE PARK ENTRANCE

RANCH

P

CULTURAL PRESERVE

	of Santa Cruz and Monterey Bay!
2.7	Pass Zane Gray Trail on the left (or take for a shorter loop option.)
3.2	Look for the singletrack shortcut trail on the left. This will lead you to the rough singletrack section of Wilder Ridge Loop known as "Horseman's Trail."
3.3	Just before you reach the sign post at the paved road, veer left on the singletrack that will parallel the road (toward the ocean) for a while. As you descend the ridge, you'll pass a landfill on the right.
4.7	Keep to the left as you ride into the fabulous section of singletrack known as the 'Dairy Mill Trail.' (On the right, the Horseman's Trail continues onto a grassy campsite area and an alternate access to Highway 1.)
5.2	Zane Gray Trail merges in from the left.
7.0	Go right as you reach the dirt road section of the Wilder Ridge Loop.
7.7	Merge right onto the dirt road, and return to the tunnel.
8.2	End of the line.

Overlooking the coastal terrace on the Wilder Ridge Loop.

Baldwin/Enchanted Loop

Blasting down the Baldwin Trail.

Location: 4 miles north of Santa Cruz on Highway 1.

Distance: 5.3+ miles.

Elevation: 30/580 ft.

Trail Surface: 79% singletrack; 21% fire road & doubletrack.

Type of Ride: Loop.

Terrain: Grasslands; oak & redwood forest; creeks; views.

Technical Level: Medium/Difficult.

Aerobic Level: Moderate/Strenuous.

Highlights: This figure-eight loop is a bit off the beaten path and provides great alternative access to the northwest side of Wilder Ranch's trail system. Uncrowded singletrack sections in the redwoods, a great workout with a massive ocean vista, fast downhills, canyon views, wildlife; this ride has it all!

Options: For an epic loop, combine with Rides 1, 4 and/or 5.

Note: The Enchanted Loop Trail is sometimes closed after major rain storms due to erosion problems.

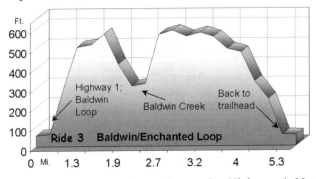

Directions/Access: In Santa Cruz, take Highway 1 North (Mission St) past the main entrance to Wilder Ranch. You'll pass a county landfill on right and farm buildings on the left. Look for a long pull-out on left, often packed with surfers' cars. Park at the far end of "4-Mile" surf spot parking on the right near a gated paved road that looks like some-one's drive way. (Just beyond, you'll see mail box # 3810 on Hwy 1). Go down the paved road

Baldwin Loop Trailhead.

past the gate and spot the trailhead just ahead on right.

Mileage Guide	
0.0	Ride down the road to the trailhead signed "Baldwin Loop Trail." (The trail on the left passes through the tunnel to Ride 1 and 4-Mile Beach.) Just ahead, you'll come to a split. Veer right and climb.
.50	Merge left onto the fire road and keep pedaling up.
1.7	After the trail plateaus, the Baldwin Loop intersects with the Enchanted Loop. Veer left onto the singletrack and

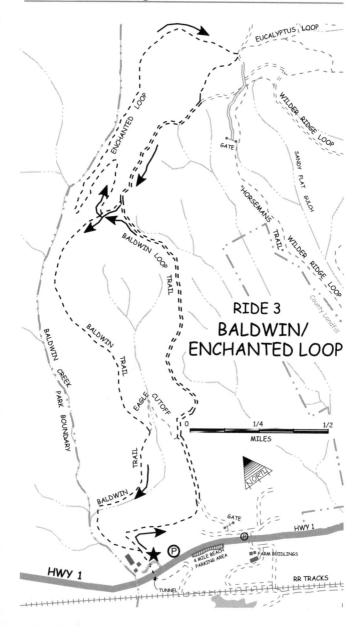

RIDE 3
BALDWIN/
ENCHANTED LOOP

	almost immediately you'll ride to another split. Turn right onto the Enchanted Trail. At first, the trail is more technical as it dashes through the rutted root tangles of the woods before flattening out near a mossy fern-lined creek in the redwood forest.
2.5	A steep eroded uphill section (in desperate need of a re-route) greets as you reemerge from the forest. Keep your eyes open in this wildlife hotspot as you crank up this quick heart-thumping hill that will certainly test your will to stay on the bike.
2.9	Old corral intersection area. Unless you want to ride additional singletrack on the Eucalyptus Loop, take the trail on the right that leads back into the forest.
3.1	Merge right onto the Enchanted fire road, which winds through open meadows framed by broad ocean vistas.
3.6	Make a right at the trail split, and then take a quick left to descend the other side of Baldwin Loop. As you dive towards the ocean, you'll pass a spectacular canyon off to the right and eventually ride into a lush ravine on smooth singletrack.
5.3	Back to the bottom of the Baldwin Loop.

Enchanting redwoods near Baldwin Creek.

Wilder Singletrack Loop

Smooth curvy groovyness.

Location: Off of Highway 1, just north of Santa Cruz.

Distance: 12.4 miles.

Elevation: 30/630 ft.

Trail Surface: 80% singletrack; 20% fire road.

Type of Ride: Loop.

Terrain: Grasslands; forest; creeks; ocean & mountain views.

Technical Level: Moderate/Difficult; some sections are steep, rocky, rutted, and/or rooted.

Exertion Level: Moderate/Strenuous; lots of changes in elevation, but most of it is gradual.

Highlights: Filled with miles of savory singletrack, this exhilarating ride is one way to maximize some of the best trails ridden in Wilder Ranch. As the ride links the sunny grassland with dense dark redwood groves and the dappled shade of oak trees, you'll enjoy pedaling Englesman, Wild Boar, Old Cabin, Eucalyptus, Enchanted loop, Twin Oaks, Zane Grey, and Dairy Mill section of Wilder Ridge Loop.

Options: Mix 'n' match the trails or lengthen the ride by adding additional singletrack options, such as Horseman's Trail or the Baldwin Loop.

Note: Multi-use trails. Although most people on the trail are bikers, watch out for hikers and equestrians.

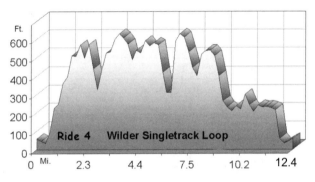

Ride 4 Wilder Singletrack Loop

Directions/Access: See Directions/Access on Ride 1.

Mileage Guide	
0.0	From the Wilder Ranch day-use parking, head down the paved road past the restrooms and turn left at the Cultural Preserve.
.30	After riding through the tunnel, keep riding straight.
.50	You'll be at an intersection with the Englesman Loop Trails, after crossing over the bridge. Take the leftmost side of the Englesman Loop.
1.8	Time for some singletrack! Go left on Wild Boar Trail.
2.2	The trail widens and curves up to the right. Up ahead, pedal left to descend into the forest on some sweet sinuous singletrack; Old Cabin Trail.
3.4	Bike left on Eucalyptus Loop Trail.

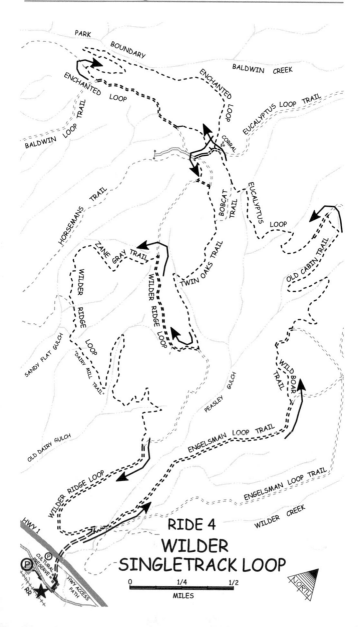

PARK BOUNDARY

BALDWIN CREEK

ENCHANTED LOOP

ENCHANTED LOOP TRAIL

BALDWIN LOOP TRAIL

EUCALYPTUS LOOP TRAIL

CORRAL

HORSEMANS TRAIL

BOBCAT TRAIL

EUCALYPTUS LOOP

ZANE GRAY TRAIL

WILDER RIDGE LOOP

TWIN OAKS TRAIL

OLD CABIN TRAIL

WILDER RIDGE LOOP

SANDY FLAT GULCH

DAIRY MILL TRAIL

WILD BOAR TRAIL

OLD DAIRY GULCH

PEASLEY GULCH

ENGELSMAN LOOP TRAIL

WILDER RIDGE LOOP

ENGELSMAN LOOP TRAIL

WILDER CREEK

HWY 1

CULTURAL PRESERVE

HWY ACCESS PATH

RR

RIDE 4
WILDER
SINGLETRACK LOOP

0   1/4   1/2

MILES

NORTH

4.3	Bobcat trail splits off after the second creek crossing; keep riding straight (right).
4.6	As you come to the end of the trail, pedal straight into the old corral area. Spot the Enchanted Loop trails just ahead to the right of the dirt road. To ride the loop clockwise, pass the first trail on the right and take the second higher trail that leads into the forest.
4.8	Veer right as you merge onto the Enchanted fire road. Scope out more incredible views ahead!
5.3	At the split, go to the right on the singletrack. (Here, the Enchanted loop tangents the Baldwin Loop). At the next split stay to the right again and get ready to rock 'n' roll through this ripping section of trail!
6.1	Bear through this short-but-brutal steep section.
6.5	Back at the old corral area. Make a right and ride up the dirt road.
6.6	Pass the Wilder Ridge fire road and take the next left onto the trail.
6.7	Veer left onto the dirt road, and look for the trail up ahead on the right. Take this; the Twin Oaks Trail.
7.1	Ignore Bobcat trail merging on the left.
7.8	Turn right. Hopefully, that descent refreshed you enough to crank up this steep incline of the Wilder Ridge Loop.
8.0	The viewpoint on the left is a great excuse to catch your breathe. Otherwise, keep rolling up the main trail.
8.5	Zane Gray Trail. Go left to descend this trail.
9.4	Merge left and traverse across the rolling hills on the Dairy Mill Trail (part of Wilder Ridge Loop Trail).
11.2	At the Wilder Ridge fire road, turn right.
11.9	Merge right at the dirt road and return the way you came.
12.4	Ride complete!

Wilder-Gray Whale Ride

Amber waves of grain on the Englesman Loop Trail.

Location: Just north of Santa Cruz off Highway 1.

Distance: 10-14 miles.

Elevation: 20/1130 ft.

Trail Surface: 100% fire roads & doubletrack.

Type of Ride: Loop; with optional out & back section.

Terrain: Sunny coastal grasslands; spectacular vistas.

Technical Level: Medium; a few steep and rutted sections.

Exertion Level: Strenuous; although a mostly gradual climb.

Highlights: Weaving throughout much of Wilder and Gray Whale Ranches, this scenery-intense loop ride makes a wonderful sunny workout on fire roads. The ride treats you to many beautiful panoramic views framing the rolling golden hills and forested ravines, as it climbs well over 1,000 feet in elevation. The ride consists of the Wilder Ridge, Eucalyptus, Chinquapin, Long Meadow, and Englesman trails, with a possible out & back section on the forested Woodcutter's Trail.

Options: Tons of options! Mix up the trails or ride into UCSC.

Note: You will pass some unauthorized trails in the area. If you'd like to see more singletrack options for mountain biking, write letters to State Parks and join local advocacy groups.

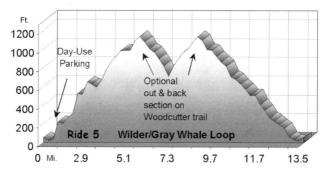

Directions/Access: See Directions/Access on Ride 1.

Mileage Guide	
0.0	From the Wilder Ranch day-use parking area, pedal from the bathrooms downhill on the paved road.
.10	Turn left at the farm buildings and head for the tunnel.
.40	Take the first major left and grind up up the Wilder Ridge Loop Trail.
1.3	Continue climbing straight ahead on the main fire road.
2.0	As you pass Twin Oaks Trail, you'll encounter one of the steepest uphill sections of the ride. Feel that burn!
2.2	An awesome viewpoint of Monterey Bay is off to the left. If you've already caught your breath, keep on the main trail (to the right). Soon you will also pass the Zane Gray Trail off to the left.
3.2	Just ahead, you will pass the top of Twin Oaks Trail as the road curves to the left.
3.4	At the road intersection, turn and pedal right
3.5	Roll on by the Enchanted Loop trails off to the left. Stay on the road as it curves around and soon you'll come to

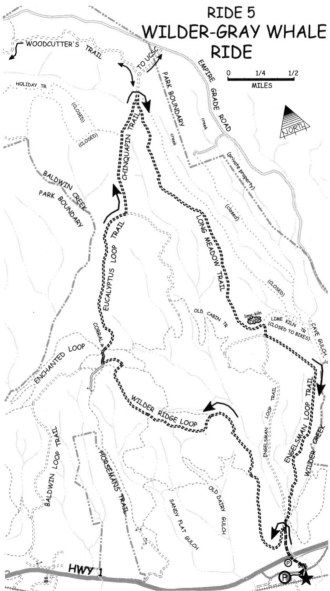

RIDE 5
WILDER-GRAY WHALE
RIDE

	the Eucalyptus Loop; stay on the main fire road here.
4.7	If you haven't grown numb to the scenery, you'll notice the vast expanses of beauty awaiting you after that climb! The nearby eucalyptus grove provides a nice picnic area. To keep riding, take a left through the open gate onto the Chinquapin Trail (dirt road).
5.6	Decision time: You can turn right onto Long Meadow trail and begin your descent. Or, you can extend your ride farther into Gray Whale Ranch on Woodcutter's Trail by riding about 4 more miles total. (Woodcutter's section is an out & back that descends to a creek. It branches off Chinquapin in about .2 miles on the left).
7.8	Toward the bottom of Long Meadow, the road bends right near the ruins of the Lime Kiln and old quarry.
7.9	After passing the ruins, you will come to a major 4-way intersection. Ride left onto Englesman Loop.
9.4	Merge straight onto the main Wilder dirt road that leads back to the tunnel.
10	After passing through the Cultural Preserve, you should be back at the main parking lot.

Riding up Long Meadow Trail near the Lime Kiln ruins.

Wilder/Gray Whale Trail Guide

Looking west towards Japan.

6A. Baldwin Loop Trail

Distance: 3.5 miles.

Elevation: 30/580 ft.

Trail Surface: 75% singletrack; 25% fire road.

Terrain: Coastal terraces; grass; rocks; oaks; canyon.

Technical Level: Medium/Difficult

Exertion Level: Moderate/Strenuous; some steep climbs.

Highlights: An uncrowded short singletrack & fire road loop with unreal ocean and canyon views.

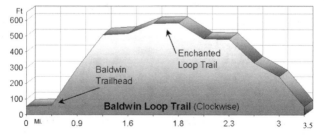

6B. Eagle Cutoff Trail

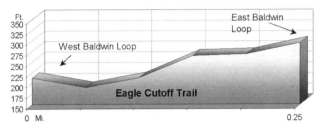

Distance: .25 miles.
Elevation: 190/290 ft.
Trail Surface: 100% singletrack.
Terrain: Open coastal terrace; gully.
Technical Level: Medium.
Exertion Level: Moderate.
Highlights: Dives into a gully bisecting the Baldwin Loop.

6C. Enchanted Loop Trail

Distance: 2 miles.
Elevation: 330/600 ft.
Trail Surface: 73% singletrack;
27% fire road.
Terrain: Grasslands; forest; creek.
Technical Level: Difficult
Exertion Level: Moderate; with
one very steep rutted segment.

Enchanted shadow biker.

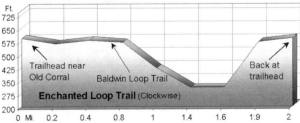

Highlights: Short loop with an insane singletrack section that darts through the "Enchanted Forest!" This trail is often closed during the rainy season and may be partially re-routed soon.

6D. Englesman Loop Trail

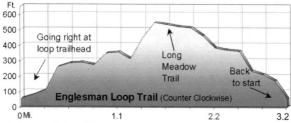

Distance: 3.2 miles.
Elevation: 50/545 ft.
Trail Surface: 100% narrow fire road.
Terrain: Coastal grasslands with forested gullies.
Technical Level: Easy/Medium.
Exertion Level: Moderate/Strenuous; steady climbing.
Highlights: With sweeping ocean views, this pleasant ride heads inland and accesses many other trails in Wilder and Gray Whale (upper Wilder Ranch).

6E. Wild Boar Trail

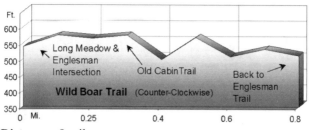

Distance: .8 miles.
Elevation: 510/575 ft.
Trail Surface: 40% singletrack; 60% fire road.
Terrain: Sparse forest and a grassy meadow.

Wild Boar is not a bore!

Technical Level: Easy/Medium.

Exertion Level: Moderate.

Highlights: Wild Boar consists of a short section of lush swoopy singletrack, and connects Englesman Loop, Long Meadow Trail, and Old Cabin Trail.

6F. Old Cabin Trail

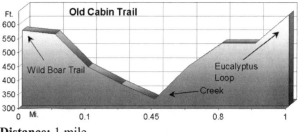

Distance: 1 mile.

Elevation: 325/630 ft.

Trail Surface: 100% singletrack.

Terrain: Forested gulch; small creek crossing.

Technical Level: Medium.

Exertion Level: Moderate.

Highlights: This flowy section of forested trail leads down to a creek and connects Wild Boar to Eucalyptus Trails.

6G. Eucalyptus Loop Trail

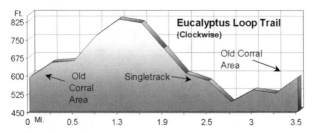

Eucalyptus picnic area.

Distance: 3.5 miles.
Elevation: 490/830 ft.
Trail Surface: 29% singletrack; 71% fire road.
Terrain: Coastal grass; some forest.
Technical Level: Medium.
Exertion Level: Moderate.
Highlights: This loop trail has some of the best panoramic ocean views in Wilder Ranch along with a superb section of singletrack that cruises through a forest of speckled light.

6H. Twin Oaks Trail

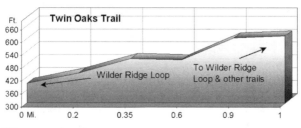

Distance: 1 mile.
Elevation: 390/615 ft.

Distance: 1 mile.
Elevation: 390/615 ft.
Trail Surface: 100% singletrack.
Terrain: Rolling grass hills with some sparse oak forest.
Technical level: Medium.
Exertion Level: Moderate.
Highlights: Twin oaks is a great singletrack alternative to one fire road section of the Wilder Ridge Loop.

6I. Bobcat Trail

Distance: .25 miles.
Elevation: 560/610 ft.
Trail Surface: 100% singletrack.

A bobcat trail enjoyed by mountain bikers.

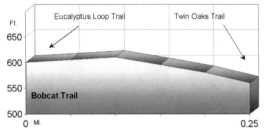

Terrain: Sparse forest.
Technical Level: Medium.
Exertion Level: Easy.
Highlights: This short glissading singletrack connects the Eucalyptus Loop singletrack to Twin Oaks Trail.

6J. Wilder Ridge Loop Trail (in 3 sections)

"Fire Road Section"

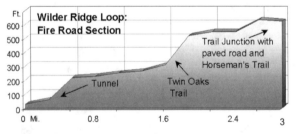

Distance: 3 miles.
Elevation: 26/620 ft.
Trail Surface: 100% fire road.
Terrain: Coastal grasslands; sparse forest; ridges.
Technical Level: Easy/Medium.
Exertion Level: Moderate/Strenuous; one very strenuous but short section.
Highlights: Since it connects many of the Wilder Ranch trails to the cultural preserve and trailhead area, this is a popular segment by default. The route has an opportune viewpoint and provides abundant access to other trail options.

"Horseman's Trail"

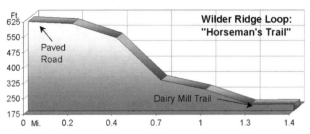

Distance: 1.4 miles.
Elevation: 200/610 ft.
Trail Surface: 100% singletrack.
Terrain: Steep coastal terraces; grassy ridges; oak trees.
Technical Level: Difficult; steep sections with ruts and bumps.
Exertion Level: Moderate riding downhill;
Very Strenuous riding uphill (not recommended).
Highlights: Get ready to rumble on this bomber descent.

"Dairy Mill Trail" ("Old Dairy Trail")

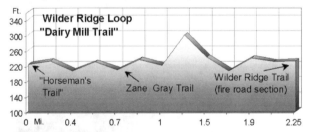

Distance: 2.3 miles.
Elevation: 200/300 ft.
Tread: 100% singletrack.
Trail Surface: Grasslands; creeks.
Technical Level: Moderate.
Exertion Level: Medium.
Highlights: This popular meandering singletrack dances in and out of ravines amidst grassy hills.

6K. Zane Gray Trail

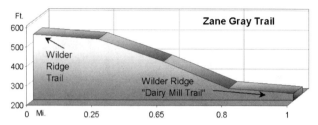

Distance: 1 mile.
Elevation: 200/300 ft.
Tread: 100% singletrack.
Trail Surface: Grassy terraced hills; forested gulch; creek.
Technical Level: Difficult; some maneuvering required.
Exertion Level: Strenuous riding uphill.
Highlights: Encircled by killer awesome coastline views, this fast trail makes both a fun descent and climb.

Inzane singletrack!

6L. Cowboy Loop Trail

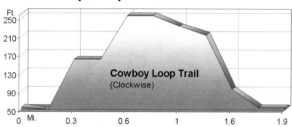

Distance: 1.9 miles.
Elevation: 55/255 ft.
Trail Surface: 100% singletrack; very rough in places.
Terrain: Grassy hills; some forest; creek crossings.
Technical Level: Medium; difficult in some sections.
Exertion Level: Moderate; with one steep strenuous section.
Highlights: The Cowboy Loop could be a good trail if more bikers rode it; however it is fairly rough with deep hoof prints.

6M. Chinquapin Trail

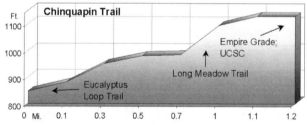

Distance: 1.2 miles.
Elevation: 850/1125 ft.
Trail Surface: 100% dirt road & doubletrack.
Terrain: Meadows; sparse forest.
Technical Level: Easy.
Exertion Level: Moderate; steady climbing.
Highlights: Connecting Wilder Ranch with UCSC, this is a lightly gravelled dirt road. The trails forming beside the road depict the intense desire for more singletrack in upper Wilder.

6N. Long Meadow Trail

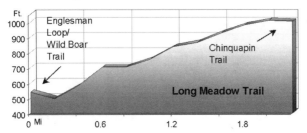

Distance: 2.3 miles.
Elevation: 500/980 ft.
Trail Surface: 100% narrow fire road.
Terrain: Grassy hills with forested canyons; ocean views.
Technical Level: Easy/medium.
Exertion Level: Moderate; steady climbing.
Highlights: As it steadily climbs toward UCSC, this pleasant fire road is a primary connecter between the upper and lower Wilder Ranch trails.

6O. Woodcutter's Trail

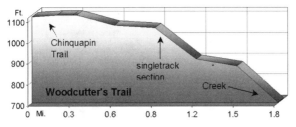

Distance: 1.8 miles one-way.
Elevation: 700/1100 ft.
Trail Surface: Narrow fire road.
Terrain: Forest; Creek.
Technical Level: Medium.
Exertion Level: Moderate/Strenuous when climbing out.
Highlights: Woodcutter's Trail is a nice forested out & back addition to upper Wilder Ranch, but lacks a loop option.

UCSC

Higher rider education.

Centrally located between Wilder Ranch, Pogonip, and Henry Cowell, the University of California Santa Cruz will draw you into this vortex of mountain biking. Although the Upper Campus area is jam-packed with sweet trails, most of them are unauthorized for biking. There are several nature reserves scattered throughout the area, in which hiking is the only permitted use on these once legally ridden trails. The residing rule states that mountain bikes are only allowed on designated dirt roads. However, the advocacy group, Mountain Bikers of Santa Cruz, has been trying to change policy and help open more trails on campus.

For now, Chinquapin Road is one of the most utilized "trails" in the upper campus. As this dirt road cuts through the length of the upper campus on its way to Wilder Ranch, it passes other roads and trails in the area. The upper campus is open for riding from 5 am through 8 pm. Dogs are not allowed.

UC SANTA CRUZ
(NORTH CAMPUS)

North Campus Loop

On the way to Shangri La.

Location: University of California, Santa Cruz.
Distance: 3.1+ miles. More miles are possible.
Elevation: 810/1035 ft.
Trail Surface: 100% fire roads.
Type of Ride: Loop.
Terrain: Shady forest.
Technical Level: Easy.
Exertion Level: Moderate.

Highlights: This network of upper campus fire roads provides a quick and convenient workout close to town. You can connect this ride to the Wilder Ranch, Pogonip, and Henry Cowell trails for longer rides, explore around or just grind out a great cardio session in the undeveloped portion of UCSC.

Options: Possibilities are endless.

Note: UCSC designates only the fire roads for mountain biking. Most of the singletrack in the area is unauthorized or part of the nature preserve. As insanely painful as it may be, this book encourages riders to acknowledge the rules.

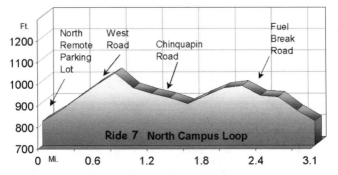

Directions/Access: Take Mission Street/Hwy 1 north and turn right on Bay Dr. Just before the campus, turn left onto Empire Grade. Next, go right on Heller Street and take this all the way up to the North Remote Parking Lot. On weekends it is free to park here. Otherwise, you will need a parking pass. Many people will park off campus to avoid the hassle of parking here while school is in session. See Also Ride 8 & 9 for other parking options.

Mileage Guide	
0.0	In the North Remote Parking Lot, ride to the north end and take the fire road, West Road You will immediately pass by the gate labeled "UCSC Upper Campus."
.40	Ride past Fuel Break Rd and North Fuel Break Road.
.80	At the water tanks, go right onto Chinquapin Rd.
1.8	Turn right on Fuel Break Road.
2.3	At the split, take either road (Fuel Break or North Fuel Break Roads).
2.7	Turn left on West Road to bomb back down.
3.1	Back at the parking lot.

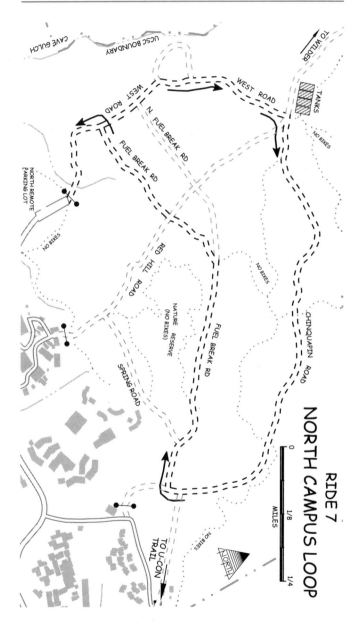

RIDE 7
NORTH CAMPUS LOOP

Cowell-Wilder Regional Trail

This trail will make you spin.

Location: 2.5 miles out of Santa Cruz on Highway 9.
Distance: 8+ miles.
Elevation: 300/1130 ft.
Trail Surface: 34% singletrack; 66% dirt & fire road.
Type of Ride: Out & Back; or Loop with UCSC trails.
Terrain: Forest; redwood groves; some open grassland.
Technical Level: Medium.
Exertion Level: Moderate; gradual climbing.

Highlights: Linking Henry Cowell, Pogonip, and UCSC to Wilder Ranch; this ride is the official designated mountain bike connector between the state parks. Along the way, the route features some of the smoothest and flowy singletrack sections in the county along with bermed-out forest fire roads.

Options: Although this ride is described as an out & back, many bikers create their own specialized loop rides using other trails in UCSC, Henry Cowell, or by crossing Empire Grade Road into Wilder Ranch. (See map). Pioneer-types will have fun exploring the area!

Note: Even though this ride passes some highly ridden single-track trails, only the dirt roads are officially open for biking on UCSC property at this time. Pray that the trails open some day since they would allow for some nice loop additions.

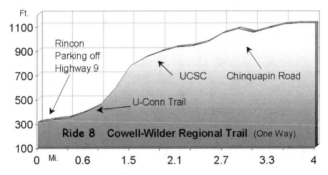

Directions/Access: From the intersection of Highways 17 and 1, go about 1 mile north on Highway 1. At the stop light at River Street, go right. This will turn into Highway 9. Take this for about 2.5 miles and park at the wide Rincon Trail pullout on the right. There is a gate with a dirt road leading down and across the train tracks. The trail is on the right just before the tracks.

U-Con do it!

Mileage Guide

0.0	From the Rincon Turnout, ride past the gate and take the trail on the right. It's signed "Rincon Connector Trail" part of the "Cowell-Wilder Regional Trail."
.10	Carefully cross Highway 9 and continue up the trail.
.60	Merge right onto the service road signed "Rincon Trail." An information panel is just ahead.
.80	Turn right onto U-Con Trail at the sign, and enjoy this swoopy serpentine singletrack on your way up to UCSC.
1.6	The UCSC information panel is at the top. Just ahead, veer right onto Fuel Break Road.
1.8	Pass around the gate and then Turn right on Chinquapin Road. A small jump/bmx area is ahead on the left.
2.8	Water Tanks and major trail intersection area. Go straight to continue on Chinquapin Road.
3.0	You will pass a series of nature reserve trails (hiking only) spurring off of Chinquapin Road.
4.0	Gate at Empire Grade Road. At this point, you may cross the road into Wilder/Gray Whale Ranch or turn around to ride back.
8.0	If you chose this ride as an Out & Back, you'll be back to the Rincon pullout now.

Studying hard at UCSC.

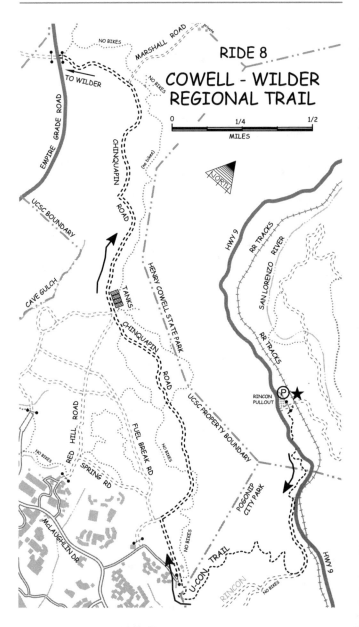

RIDE 8
COWELL - WILDER REGIONAL TRAIL

Arroyo Seco-UCSC-Wilder Loop

Artistic tanks marking a major intersection of trails at UCSC.

Location: Santa Cruz; near Swift Street.
Distance: 14+ miles.
Elevation: 30/1130 ft.
Trail Surface: 22% singletrack; 48% fire & dirt roads; 21% paved bike path; 9% paved road.
Type of Ride: Loop.
Terrain: Forest; grasslands; creeks; ocean views; UCSC.
Technical Level: Medium.
Exertion Level: Strenuous; a good amount of climbing.

Highlights: This excellent loop ride from town heads up Arroyo Seco canyon, through UCSC, down Gray Whale and Wilder Ranch, and back along the County Bike Path. The Arroyo Seco section is an enjoyable alternative to riding up Bay Street for access to the UCSC trails.

Options: There are many ways to tweak this ride to fit your wildest desires. With a variety of trails in UCSC, Gray Whale and Wilder, you have ample ability to pick and choose trails. The described ride is only one suggestion, as well as the most direct.

Note: Just another reminder that bikes are not allowed on the UCSC Nature Preserve trails.

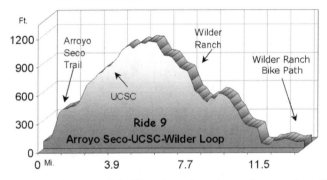

Directions/Access: Take Hwy 1 north to the northwest edge of the city. Turn left at Shaffer Rd. and park on the side of the road near the bike path crossing.

Mileage Guide	
0.0	From Shaffer Drive/Bike Path, ride across to Mission St. Ext. and take the bounded bike lane.
.30	Turn left on Western Drive and cross Highway 1. Then take an immediate right on Grand View Drive (closed to cars on this side).
.70	As you ride down Grand View Dr, look for a small park on the left. Take the trail/path that starts between the chain link fence and stucco wall to the right of the small private park. (Do not actually go into the park).
.80	Cross the bridge over creek and follow the trail into the Eucalyptus grove.
.90	After another bridge, the trail heads left and becomes a wider path now.

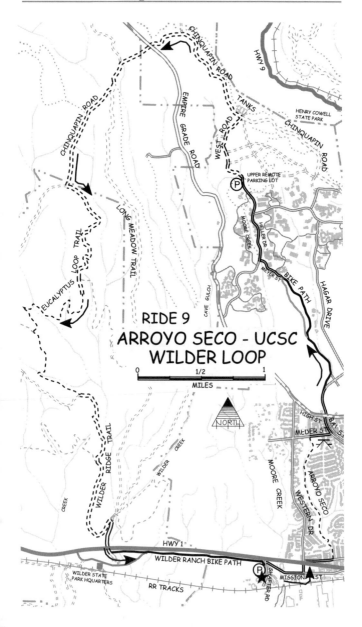

CHINQUAPIN ROAD

HWY 9

HENRY COWELL STATE PARK

CHINQUAPIN ROAD

EMPIRE GRADE ROAD

CHINQUAPIN ROAD

WEST ROAD

TANKS

UPPER REMOTE PARKING LOT

LONG MEADOW TRAIL

MOORE CREEK

HELLER DR.

MEDER ST

EUCALYPTUS LOOP TRAIL

CAVE GULCH

BIKE PATH

HAGAR DRIVE

RIDE 9
ARROYO SECO - UCSC
WILDER LOOP

0   1/2   1

MILES

NORTH

HIGH ST

BAY ST

MEDER ST

WILDER CREEK

WILDER RIDGE TRAIL

MOORE CREEK

ARROYO SECO

WESTERN DR.

CREEK

HWY 1

WILDER RANCH BIKE PATH

WILDER STATE PARK HQUARTERS

RR TRACKS

SHAFFER RD

MISSION ST

1.2	Split. Go left and pedal up the gradual incline.
1.5	The trail becomes paved; keep riding straight to the park.
1.8	Steer right on Meder Street and ride to Bay Street.
2.0	Turn left on Bay Street and ride up the bike lane.
2.2	After crossing High Street, ride into UCSC. Stay on the same road until you reach the top of the hill.
2.5	At the stoplight, turn left toward the "Farm" area. Just after this turn, spot the green sign and take the paved bike path on your right.
3.5	Bike path ends. Pedal straight on Meyer Street, passing two stop signs.
3.7	Major Intersection at Heller St. Across the street, there is a trail that leads up to the upper campus trails. However, it is now part of the UCSC Nature Reserve and officially off limits to bikes. This may change in the future, hopefully, with the efforts of MBOSC. Unless trail policies change, go right on Heller Street. (There is a little trail paralleling the right side of the road for avoiding the traffic).
4.1	At the intersection, with a parking structure on the right, continue straight ahead on Heller St.
4.4	After riding straight through the parking area, veer left on the dirt road, West Road. Ride around the gate labeled "UCSC Upper Campus" and continue up.
5.5	When you come to the open space at the tanks, go left on Chinquapin dirt road.
6.4	Gate. Cross Empire Grade and ride past the gate into Wilder Ranch. Continue on Chinquapin or take any of the options in Wilder Ranch to descend back to the Wilder Ranch Cultural Preserve/Tunnel. (See Rides 1-6).
12.5	Just after passing through the Hwy 1 tunnel, turn left on the Wilder Ranch Bike Path that parallels Highway 1 South.
14+	Back at Shaffer Dr. End of loop.

UCSC Trail Guide

The Upper Campus forest beckons.

10A. Chinquapin Road (UCSC side)

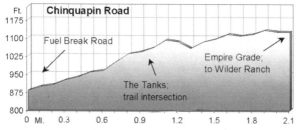

Distance: 2.1 miles.

Elevation: 880/1130 ft.

Trail Surface: 100% dirt road.

Terrain: Forest; meadows.

Technical Level: Easy.

Exertion Level: Moderate.

Highlights: Providing access to many other trails in the area, this widely used road is the main link between Pogonip and Wilder Ranch.

10B. Fuel Break Road

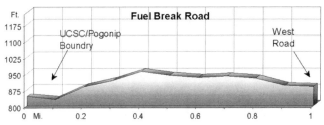

Distance: 1 mile.
Elevation: 830/958 ft.
Trail Surface: 100% dirt road.
Terrain: Forest.
Technical Level: Easy.
Exertion Level: Moderate.
Highlights: Fuel Break is another widely used road that cuts through the upper campus and meets up with Chinquapin Road near Pogonip.

10C. North Fuel Break Road

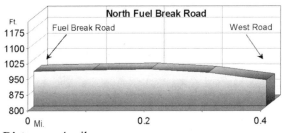

Distance: .4 miles.
Elevation: 925/980 ft.
Trail Surface: 100% dirt road.
Terrain: Forest; chaparral.
Technical Level: Easy.
Exertion Level: Moderate.
Highlights: A short segment, this road is an offshoot and parallels Fuel Break Road.

10D. West Road

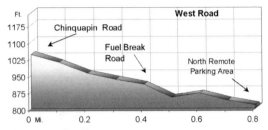

Distance: .8 miles.
Elevation: 820/1040 ft.
Trail Surface: 100% dirt road.
Terrain: Forest; chaparral.
Technical Level: Easy.
Exertion Level: Moderate/ Strenuous.
Highlights: West road directly links the campus parking area to Chinquapin and Fuel Break Roads near the water tanks.

10E. Red Hill Road

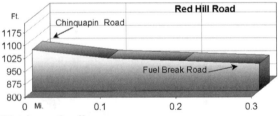

Distance: .3 miles.
Elevation: 960/1050 ft.
Trail Surface: 100% dirt road.
Terrain: Forest.
Technical Level: Easy.
Exertion Level: Moderate.
Highlights: This dirt road parallels West Road and bisects North Fuel Break and Fuel Break Roads. The lower section of this road near the campus is off limits to bikes for some reason.

Pogonip Park

Trails this great actually do exist beyond our dreams.

Pogonip is a City of Santa Cruz Greenbelt Park with a scenic 640-acre expanse of open meadows, woodlands, and creeks. While mountain bike trails are limited in number, there is one fabulous route open. Providing non-stop biking access from Henry Cowell to UCSC, this mostly-singletrack section includes Rincon Connector Trail, Rincon Road, and the U-Con Trail.

The park is open from sunrise to 7 pm in the summer, and until 4 pm in the winter. Located between UCSC and highway 9, the mountain bike parking is at the Rincon Pullout about 2.5 miles north of Santa Cruz. Leashed dogs are permitted on the Rincon Trail, but not the Rincon Connector or Ucon Trails.

The U-Con Trail
(with Rincon Connector Trail)

All "alone" on the U-Con Trail.

Location: 2.5 miles north of Santa Cruz on Highway 9.
Distance: 3.2 miles roundtrip.
Elevation: 310/840 ft.
Trail Surface: 85% singletrack; 15% narrow fire road.
Terrain: Redwood forest.
Type of Ride: Out & Back.
Technical Difficulty: Easy/Medium.
Exertion Level: Easy/Moderate; due to its short length.

Highlights: For a quick fix, the U-Con Trail is a superb short ride on some of the most smooth-to-the-groove singletrack around. This trail is a great introduction to singletrack for new mountain bikers, while more experienced riders will want to ride further into UCSC and/or Wilder Ranch.

Options: For a longer ride, see Ride 8.

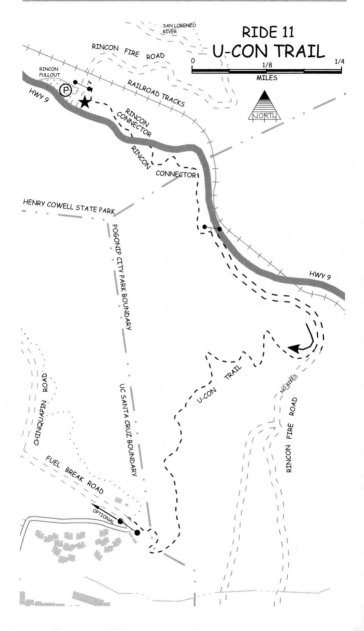

RIDE 11
U-CON TRAIL

Note: Have fun!

U-Con Trail & Rincon Connector Trail (One Way)

[Elevation profile chart: Ft. on vertical axis (100 to 900), Mi. on horizontal axis (0 to 1.6). Labels: "Rincon Parking off Highway 9", "U-Con Trailhead", "UCSC Sign". Horizontal axis marks: 0, 0.2, 0.4, 0.6, 0.9, 1.3, 1.5, 1.6]

Directions/Access:

From the intersection of Highways 17 and 1, go about 1 mile north on Highway 1. At the stop light at River Street, go right.

This will turn into Highway 9. Take this for about 2.5 miles and park at the wide "Rincon Parking" pullout on the right. There is a gate there with a dirt road leading down and across the train tracks. The trail is on the right before the tracks.

Carve this wave of a trail!

Mileage Guide	
0.0	At the Rincon Turnout, ride down past the state park gate and take the trail on the right (before you come to the railroad tracks). It's signed "Rincon Connector Trail."
.10	Carefully cross Highway 9.
.60	Merge right onto the service road signed "Rincon Trail."
.80	Turn right onto U-Con Trail at the sign.
1.6	At the top is a UCSC information panel. You can keep riding into UCSC, or turn around for some swoopy downhill fun!
3.2	Back at parking lot.

Henry Cowell Redwoods State Park

Pilgrimage through an old-growth sanctuary.

If you enjoy big trees, Henry Cowell is the place to bike. The main park area contains 1,750 acres of large old-growth redwoods. Within this massive congregation of trees is a redwood that is 285 feet tall and about 16 feet wide. Having sprouted during the era of the Roman Empire, some of these trees are 1400 to 1800 years old. In addition to redwood groves, the park is filled with douglas fir, madrone, oak, some ponderosa pine. Another major highlight is the picturesque San Lorenzo River, which flows through the park on its way to the ocean.

With 20 miles of trails, the park is filled with hikers, horseback riders, and bikers. While the singletrack trails are closed to mountain bikes, cycling is permitted on Pipeline Road, Rincon Fire Road, Ridge Fire Road, and Powder Mill Fire Road. Leashed dogs are permitted on Pipeline Road.

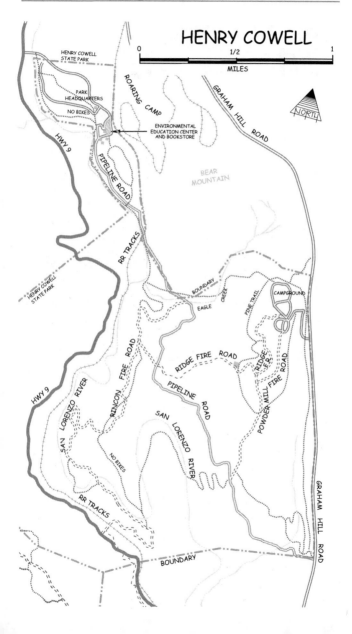

Henry Cowell Loop

A fun downhill section of old fire road.

Location: 6 miles north of Santa Cruz off highway 9.

Distance: 5.6 - 8.3 miles; depending on options chosen.

Elevation: 240/740 ft.

Trail Surface: 58% narrow fire road; 42% paved fire road.

Type of Ride: Loop with an optional out & back section.

Terrain: Redwood groves; San Lorenzo River.

Technical Level: Moderate; one deep sandy area. The ride is a bit more difficult when riding the optional section down to

the river on Rincon Fire Road. (This involves a steeper section with more rocks and ruts).
Exertion Level: Strenuous; some steep sections.

Highlights: Providing a wonderful workout on mostly smooth fire roads, this ride has some truly great scenery and beautiful access to the river. This is an adventure-type ride with everything from tire sucking sand, sections of deep horse hoof trenches, ocean views, a river, observation deck... Be ready for anything!

Options: You can ride an out & back section on Rincon Fire Road to the river; see the Mileage Guide below for details.

Note: There is no bridge over the river, but it can be crossed at low flows in the summer by wading. Use caution; its not the easiest crossing!

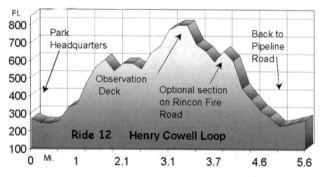

Directions/Access: Take Highway 1 into Santa Cruz. At the stop light at River Street in Santa Cruz, go right (inland) onto Hwy 9. About 6 miles later, you'll see the main entrance to Henry Cowell on the right. Parking is $7. To avoid this fee, you can park in the pullout on Hwy 9 just before the entrance road. The main parking and visitor center is about .6 miles past the entrance.

Mileage Guide	
0.0	From the parking lot near the visitor center, take one of the paved trails down to Pipeline Road.

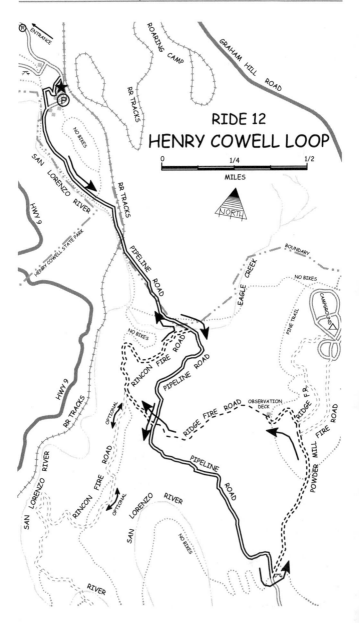

RIDE 12
HENRY COWELL LOOP

0   1/4   1/2
MILES

NORTH

.10	Pipeline Road. At the main sign, go straight. (The river will be on your right).
1.1	Keep cranking up the steep hill past Rincon Fire Road.
1.6	Bike beyond the Ridge Fire Road turnoff and spot the viewpoint up ahead on the right!
2.4	Veer left at the picnic area onto Powder Mill Fire Road.
2.9	Go straight, ignoring the road on the right that leads to the campground.
3.0	At Ridge Road, ride left up to the observation deck.
3.2	Observation Deck. If its a clear day, enjoy the panoramic ocean and forested mountain views. Continuing on the fire road, stay to the left through a sandy section and head down the backside. The next .4 miles contain several water-bar drop-offs and may be very sandy (at least its downhill!)
3.8	Cross Pipeline Road and keep going on Ridge Fire Rd.
4.0	Rincon Fire Road. To add another 2.7 miles, go left and ride an out & back section down to the river (or a shorter section to the Cathedral Redwoods). For more information on this section see the Ride 13 Mileage Guide (Miles 1.3-2.7). Otherwise, turn right to finish the loop.
4.5	Go left on Pipeline Road.
5.6	That's all folks; you're back at the main parking area.

The observation deck, a popular rest stop, has panoramic views, an information kiosk, and a drinking fountain.

Redwoods to Coast Ride

Descending to the San Lorenzo River on Rincon Fire Road.

Location: Off Graham Hill Rd, 3 miles from Santa Cruz.

Distance: 15.6 miles one-way; 32+ miles as a loop.

Elevation: 50/1130 ft.

Trail Surface: 30% singletrack; 70% dirt & fire road.

Type of Ride: One-Way shuttle; or an Loop/Out & Back for the hardcore.

Terrain: Redwood forest; San Lorenzo River; grasslands; coastal cliffs; huge ocean views!

Technical Level: Difficult; various trail conditions, some steep rocky segments, ruts, sand, river crossing.

Exertion Level: Strenuous (1-way shuttle); Very Strenuous (loop).

Highlights: This epic ride encompasses the full variety of trails in Santa Cruz. Combining Henry Cowell, Pogonip, UCSC, and Wilder Ranch, it takes you all the way from the redwoods of Felton, across the San Lorenzo River, and on to the crashing surf below the cliffs. During this ride you will enjoy the huge spectrum of terrain that Santa Cruz has to offer.

Options: There are many other trails to substitute on the way down, particularly in Wilder Ranch. If you're in a superhero mood, ride it as a loop or out & back.

Note: This ride has one of the biggest river crossings in Santa Cruz and is not recommended in the winter and spring due to high flow. The river should be avoided unless the water levels are down. Please use sound judgment before crossing.

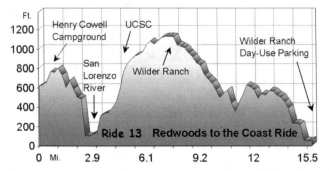

Directions/Access: The shuttle drop-off at Wilder Ranch involves driving a couple miles north of Santa Cruz on Highway 1, and leaving a car in the state park day-use parking ($6). You may also park in the dirt pullout on Highway 1 just before the main entrance or at the bike path on Shaffer Dr (Ride 32).

The ride begins at Henry Cowell State Park. From Ocean Street in Santa Cruz (off of Highway 1, by the intersection of Highway 17), go right onto Graham Hill Road. After about 3 miles, turn left into Henry Cowell Park/Campground and drive to the entrance booth. There is a fee for parking when the booth is staffed. You can park near the booth or .1 mile further up on the left by the Powder Mill trailhead.

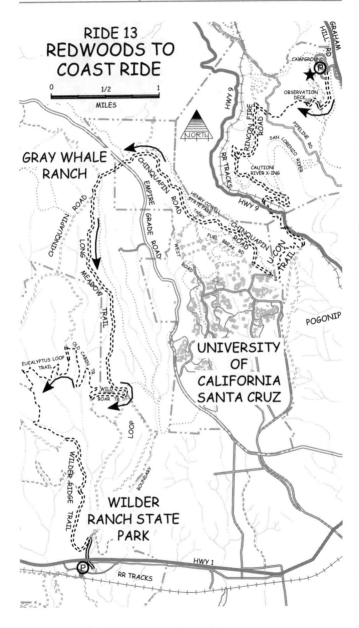

RIDE 13
REDWOODS TO
COAST RIDE

0   1/2   1
MILES

NORTH

GRAHAM HILL RD

CAMPGROUND

OBSERVATION DECK

PIPELINE RD

RINCON FIRE ROAD

SAN LORENZO RIVER

HWY 9

RR TRACKS

CAUTION! RIVER X-ING

GRAY WHALE RANCH

CHINQUAPIN ROAD

EMPIRE GRADE ROAD

HENRY COWELL STATE PARK TRAILS

CHINQUAPIN ROAD

FUEL BREAK RD

WEST ROAD

U-CON TRAIL

CHINQUAPIN ROAD

LONG MEADOW TRAIL

POGONIP

EUCALYPTUS LOOP TRAIL

OLD CABIN TR.

WILD BOAR TR.

LOOP

UNIVERSITY
OF
CALIFORNIA
SANTA CRUZ

WILDER RIDGE TRAIL

BOUNDARY

WILDER
RANCH STATE
PARK

HWY 1

RR TRACKS

New-school travel through old-growth forest.

Mileage Guide

0.0	From the Powder Mill Trailhead, ride around the gate onto the fire road.
.40	At the signed intersection, go right onto Ridge Fire Rd.
.60	Observation Deck with panoramic views! Continuing on the fire road, stay to the left and head down the backside. The next .4-mile section is one big sand trap in the summer, with many water-bar drop offs.
1.1	Cross Pipeline Road and keep going on Ridge Fire Rd.
1.3	Go left on Rincon Fire Road and ride all the way to the river. Soon you will ride through the grove known as the "Cathedral Redwoods."
2.2	The fire road will steepen as it drops to the river.
2.7	San Lorenzo River. After crossing (summertime only), spot the trail on the other side. Stay straight on the path as it leads into the fire road toward the left. The road will follow the river before weaving its way up the cliff.
3.5	Are you ready for some singletrack?! Cross the train tracks and take Rincon Connector Trail on the left.
3.6	Cross Highway 9 and continue on the trail.
4.1	Merge onto the fire road signed "Rincon Trail," heading to the right and then turn right onto U-Con Trail ahead.
5.1	Soon after the UCSC information panel at the top, you

	will see bike trails veering off. The only sanctioned bike route is to merge right onto Fuel Break Rd.
5.4	Turn right on Chinquapin Rd and pedal a couple miles.
7.5	Twin Gates at Empire Grade Road. Cross over into Wilder Ranch and continue on Chinquapin Rd. Entering Wilder Ranch will open a plethora of trail choices (See Rides 1-6). The following description is just one option:
8.0	Turn left onto Long Meadow Trail.
10.2	Stay on Long Meadow through the old quarry ruins.
10.3	Major Intersection! Go right on Wild Boar trail.
10.6	Turn right onto Old Cabin Trail for some fun singletrack.
11.6	Turn left onto Eucalyptus Loop Trail.
12.6	After crossing the creek, take Bobcat Trail on the left.
12.9	Merge left into Twin Oaks Trail.
13.6	Veer left onto Wilder Ridge Loop and take this all the way down.
15.1	Go right when you reach the turn-off at the bottom, and head past the information panel toward the tunnel.
15.4	After crossing under the tunnel, walk your bikes through the Cultural Preserve. When you come to the main paved access road, go right and ride up to the parking lot
15.6	Wilder Ranch day-use parking area.

*Commencing in thick forest, the "Redwoods to Coast Ride"
ends with mind blowing ocean views.*

Henry Cowell Trail Guide

14A. Rincon Connector Trail

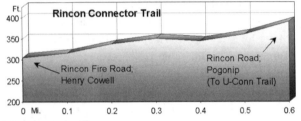

Distance: .6 miles.
Elevation: 305/390 ft.
Trail Surface: 100% singletrack.
Terrain: Forest; Highway 9 crossing.
Technical Level: Easy/Moderate.
Exertion Level: Mild.
Highlights: This flowy trail connects Rincon Road in Henry Cowell to Pogonip, UCSC, and Wilder Ranch.

14B. Rincon Fire Road

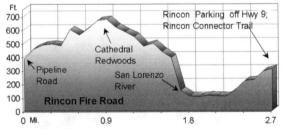

Distance: 2.7 miles.
Elevation: 100/670 ft.
Trail Surface: 100% narrow fire road.
Terrain: Redwood groves; San Lorenzo River crossing.

Rincon Reconnaissance.

Technical Level: Medium with Difficult steep and rock-strewn section descending near the river.

Exertion Level: Moderate/Strenuous.

Highlights: Connecting Pipeline and Ridge Roads to the Rincon Parking area on highway 9, this road winds through the "Cathedral Redwoods" down to the river (no bridge).

14C. Ridge Fire Road

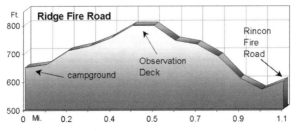

Distance: 1.1 miles.

Elevation: 570/800 ft.

Trail Surface: 100% fire road.

Terrain: Forest; observation deck with panoramic views.

Technical Level: Medium; some sand and water bar drops.

Exertion Level: Moderate.

Highlights: Connecting to Pipeline, Powder Mill, and Rincon Roads, the 360-degree views make it well worth the pedal.

14D. Powder Mill Fire Road

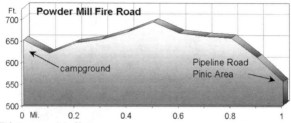

Distance: 1 mile.

Elevation: 555/690 ft.

Trail Surface: 100% fire road.

Terrain: Dense forest; campground; picnic area.

Technical Level: Easy.

Exertion Level: Moderate.

Highlights: Cruising from the campground to the Pipeline Road picnic area, this fire road also connects with Ridge Fire Road near the observation deck:

14E. Pipeline Road

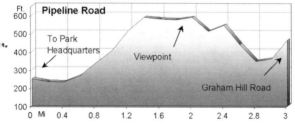

Distance: 3 miles.

Elevation: 250/590 ft.

Trail Surface: 100% paved fire road.

Terrain: San Lorenzo River; redwoods; viewpoint.

Technical Level: Easy.

Exertion Level: Moderate/Strenuous; easy near the river.

Highlights: This bike path bisects the park to provide access to many trails between Highway 9 and Graham Hill Road.

DeLaveaga Park

Airing over a big root on the Figure 8 Loop.

Although the singletrack mileage is fairly limited, DeLaveaga is a little Santa Cruz singletrack gem! Thanks to the immense generosity of Jose DeLaveaga in 1894, there's a superb chunk of open space dedicated to nothing but recreation. A challenging golf course, a world class disc golf course, an archery course, athletic fields, playgrounds….and, some sweet singletrack! While many of the trails are relatively short, there is plenty of exploration to be had. Riders of all skill levels will love DeLaveaga Park, whether you want a short family cruiser, a fast rollercoaster singletrack, or a steeper downhiller-style ride. DeLaveaga is part of the City of Santa Cruz Parks & Recreation Department. It is open for biking from 7 am to Sunset in the winter and from 7 am to 11 pm in the summer. Leashed dogs are allowed on trails.

Top of The World Trail

Happiness is found riding the Top of the World Trail.

Location: In Santa Cruz off of Branciforte Street.

Distance: 4.8+ miles.

Elevation: 120/450 ft.

Trail Surface: 77% singletrack; 23% fire road.

Type of Ride: Out & back or Loop.

Terrain: Forest; disc golf; golf course; great views.

Technical Level: Medium; mostly smooth with some random drop-offs and scattered root obstacles.

Exertion Level: Moderate.

Highlights: Glissading along groovy singletrack and forested berms on the way to the pacific-framed Top of the World lookout, this twisty ride will put a smiley face on riders of all abilities!

Options: Combine with the Figure 8 Loop for a bigger ride. Have an adventure day, and bring your frisbees for disc golf!

Note: Trails are not signed.

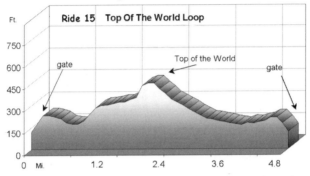

Directions/Access: From Highway 17 or 1, take "Ocean St./Beaches" exit. Get in the left-hand turn lane, and go left at the very first light on Plymouth Drive. Then take a quick right on Grant Street and follow the road down. When you reach Market Street, take a left and go under the freeway. The road will become Branciforte Dr. After passing the first stop sign, look for the dirt parking lot on the right about 500 feet ahead. The ride starts at the gate on the far side of the pullout.

Mileage Guide	
0.0	Pedal around the gate and head up the fire road.
.10	On the left is a superb singletrack option. This trail will parallel and meet up with the fire road at the .8-mile mark on this Mileage Guide.
.80	On the left, a trail (Ride 16) merges with the fire road.
.90	Major intersection area! Up the hillside on the right, there is access to the upper trails (see Ride 16). On the left, another fire road descends to Branciforte Drive and intersects more trails. Keep pedaling up the main fire road just beyond this intersection area and look for the unsigned trail on the left (La Corona Trail), which leads to Top of the World.

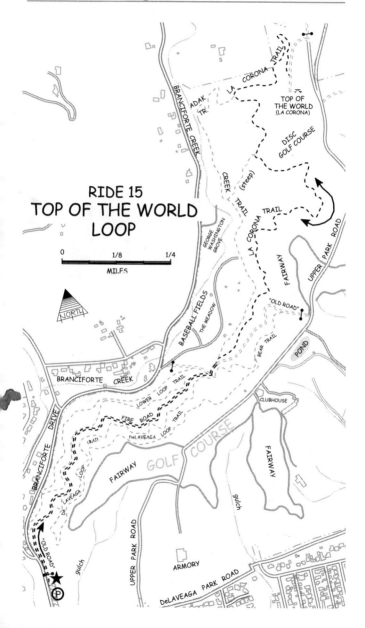

RIDE 15
TOP OF THE WORLD
LOOP

0   1/8   1/4
MILES

NORTH

1.8	Park bench and viewpoint on the left. A steep and rough trail descends to the creek trail down below.
2.0	Stay to the right as you keep pedaling up. On the left, the Adak Trail descends to the creek. This is one possible loop option (see map).
2.4	As you reach the top plateau area, ride up a little further to the right until you see the ocean framed backdrop of Monterey Bay encompass your field of view. This is Top of the World and disc golf hole #27. For the remainder of the ride, you can return the way you came or take the Adak Trail and/or part of Ride 16 to bike a loop.
4.8+	Back at the entrance gate.

Fat tire fun.

Figure 8 Loop

Cruisin' DeLaveaga Style!

Location: In Santa Cruz off of Branciforte Drive.

Miles: 3.5 miles.

Elevation: 120/310 ft.

Trail Surface: 98% singletrack; 2% fire road.

Type of Ride: Loop.

Terrain: Forest; golf course; steep slopes; some big roots.

Technical Level: Medium; mostly smooth with occasional technical sections and large roots.

Exertion Level: Moderate.

Highlights: Maximizing much of the singletrack in DeLaveaga Park, this double loop ride thrills you with flowing trails curving throughout the forest. Bikers will have fun just cruising around, while others may be enticed to hit the trails at full speed.

Options: Ride in different directions. For a longer ride, combine with Ride 15 or any of the other DeLaveaga trails.

Note: The trails are unsigned and may be slightly confusing at first... good thing you have this guide book! You'll pass close to the golf course. Respect the golfers; they carry clubs and long range projectiles.

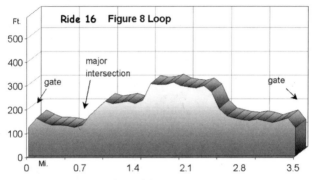

Directions/Access: See Ride 15.

Mileage Guide	
0.0	Pedal around the gate and ride up the fire road.
.10	Go left on the unmarked singletrack. Fun, fun, and more fun is just ahead!
.20	Stay to left at the split.
.70	The trail ends as you reach the fire road. Go right and ride up the road to the intersection.
.80	Main intersection. Veer a little to the right and ride up the hillside bank in front of you. Take the trail which switchbacks its way up and eventually heads to the right (ignore the other trail that merges on the left).
1.3	Huge tree roots are blocking the route; either a mega bunny hop or a quick dismount is necessary.
1.6	Stay on the main trail as it curves around and parallels the golf course, and keep it rollin'.
2.4	Make a sharp left here! (The trail to the right leads to an

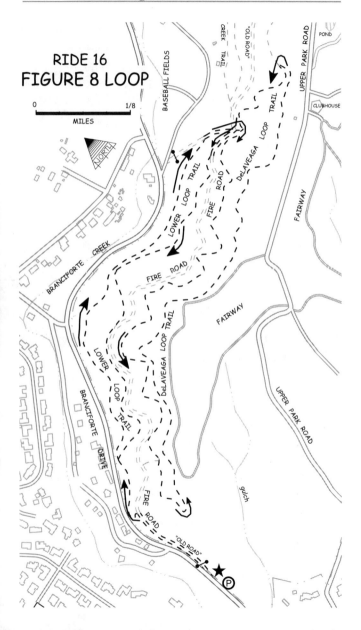

RIDE 16
FIGURE 8 LOOP

0   1/8
MILES

NORTH

BASEBALL FIELDS

CREEK TRAIL

"OLD ROAD"

UPPER PARK ROAD

POND

CLUBHOUSE

DeLAVEAGA LOOP TRAIL

LOWER LOOP TRAIL

FIRE ROAD

FAIRWAY

BRANCIFORTE CREEK

FIRE ROAD

DeLAVEAGA LOOP TRAIL

FAIRWAY

LOWER LOOP TRAIL

BRANCIFORTE DRIVE

UPPER PARK ROAD

gulch

FIRE ROAD

"OLD ROAD"

P

	intersection higher up on the main fire road.)
2.5	As you reach the switchbacks again, make a sharp right to head down.
2.6	Back at the major intersection, turn left and ride on the main fire road for a couple hundred feet. Then take the singletrack dropping off to the right.
3.2	Keep heading straight as the lower trail merges.
3.4	Once again you're at the main fire road. If you're ready to call it a day, turn right and head down to the gate.
3.5	Loop complete. Return to parking area.

Spokes among the oaks.

Forest of Nisene Marks State Park

Mountain biker paradise in lower Nisene Marks.

With 10,000 acres of rugged terrain stretching from sea level to lush 2600-foot mountains, The Forest of Nisene Marks lives up to its reputation as a premier mountain biking destination. This area has produced and is home to some of the best mountain bikers in the world, such as Cam McCaul and Jamie Goldman.

Although only some of the 30+ miles of smooth-as-silk trails are legal for bikers; the fabulous viewpoints, redwood forest, perennial creeks, and tacky soil make mountain biking here a magnificent experience. A giant "thank you" goes out to the Marks family, who donated the land to the public in 1963.

"Lower Nisene," the area below the steel bridge, contains some great bike-legal singletrack. Here, Aptos Creek Fire Road commences and scenically winds its way up through the entire length of the park. Beyond the steel bridge in "Upper Nisene," bikes are currently only allowed on the fire roads. Park management was considering the possibility of opening more trails to mountain biking, such as a Hinckley Ridge connector and West Ridge Trail. However, a lawsuit attempting to ban mountain bikes has temporarily shot down this hope. If you would like to see more ridable singletrack, please voice your opinions!

This is a high-use park filled with many bikers, as well as joggers, hikers, and horseback riders. Please, help the mountain biking cause by being courteous to all the other trail users.

Besides biking, Nisene Marks offers many interesting side excursions as well. As you ride around, you'll encounter evidence of century-old logging operations, mill sites, trestles, and the occasional Sasquatch throughout the park. Other interesting features include several impressive waterfalls, the Loma Prieta Earthquake Epicenter and the Advocate, a giant redwood with a 45-foot circumference. In addition, the park contains a backpacker camp and many picnic areas.

The main entrance is located 6 miles southeast of Santa Cruz off of Soquel Drive in Aptos. Day-use parking near the entrance booth on Aptos Creek Road costs $6. To avoid this fee, many people park down in Aptos Village at the base of the park, or ride in from another trailhead (see Ride 17 & 18) . Expert level dirt jumps are located nearby behind the Aptos post office (see page 171). Dogs must be on a leash and are allowed along Aptos Creek Fire Road (up to the Porter Picnic area) and some of the bike trails.

The joy overwhelms in Nisene Marks.

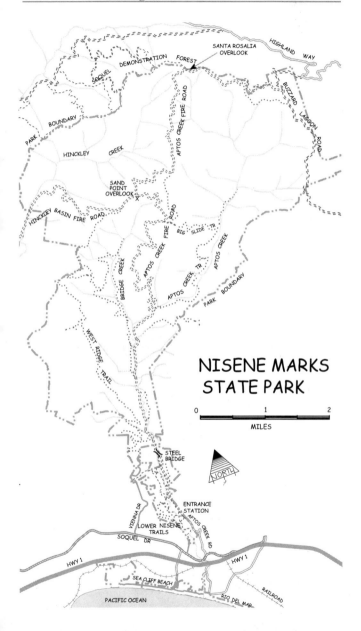

Aptos Rancho Trail

A classic Santa Cruz scene.

Location: Aptos; about 6 miles southeast of Santa Cruz.
Distance: 4 miles.
Elevation: 55/180 ft.
Trail Surface: Mostly wide singletrack.
Type of Ride: Out & Back; many loop rides are possible.
Terrain: Redwood forest; creek views; creek crossing.

Technical Level: Medium; some short eroded sections with occasional deadfall and a large tree-root booby trap.

Exertion Level: Easy/Moderate.

Highlights: As is typical of biking the Lower Nisene rides, you will encounter lush forest scenery along Aptos Creek which meanders through moss and fern covered banks below the trail. Rating high on the fun factor, this ride is a nice transitional ride for beginner/intermediate bikers, while more advanced riders will want to use this trail to access the other rides in Nisene Marks.

Options: Loops are possible with Aptos Creek Fire Road or Terrace Trail, and/or Ride 18.

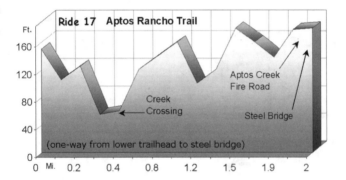

Note: Creek crossings are not recommended at higher flows. Also, be cautious of hikers and joggers who often use this trail.

Directions/Access: From Santa Cruz, take Hwy 1 south to State Park Dr. exit (# 435) in Aptos. Go inland (left); then take a right onto Soquel Drive. As you enter the Aptos Village area, make a left on Aptos Creek Rd. You can park near the trailhead, just past the entrance booth ($6 self-pay). Or, many people prefer to park behind the Aptos Station near the boundary of Nisene Marks (additional .6 miles each way). If you are riding from town, you can take Aptos Rancho Road (opposite Safeway) directly to the lower Aptos Rancho Trailhead.

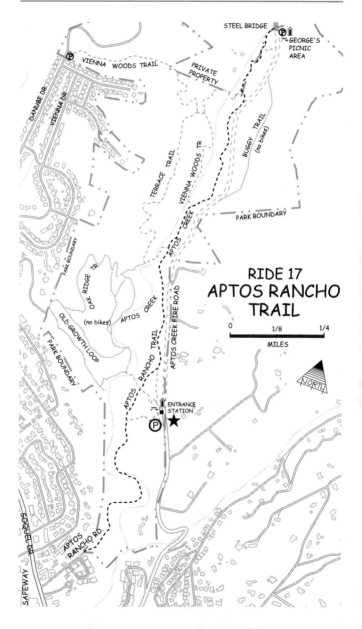

STEEL BRIDGE

GEORGE'S PICNIC AREA

VIENNA WOODS TRAIL

DANUBE DR

VIENNA DR

PRIVATE PROPERTY

TERRACE TRAIL

VIENNA WOODS TR

BUGGY TRAIL (no bikes)

APTOS CREEK

PARK BOUNDARY

OAK RIDGE TR

PARK BOUNDARY

OLD-GROWTH LOOP

APTOS CREEK

(no bikes)

APTOS RANCHO TRAIL

APTOS CREEK FIRE ROAD

RIDE 17
APTOS RANCHO TRAIL

0   1/8   1/4
MILES

NORTH

ENTRANCE STATION

PARK BOUNDARY

SOQUEL DR

APTOS RANCHO RD.

SAFEWAY

Mileage Guide

0.0	At the Kiosk and signed trailhead, take Split Stuff Trail and/or any of the connectors to Aptos Rancho Trail, where you can veer right to ride up the trail.
.50	Pedal by Terrace Trail (a possible loop option).
.60	After passing Vienna Woods Trail, continue up the hill.
.90	Nice 2-foot ego-tester root drop!
1.0	Roll on by the upper section of Terrace Trail off to the left.
1.3	George's Picnic Area.
1.4	Aptos Creek Road. The Steel Bridge is to your left. If you're riding this as an out & back, turn around and cruise back the way you came.
2.8	As you return to the intersection with Split Stuff Trail near the entrance booth, you can stay on the Aptos Rancho Trail to keep riding an additional out & back section.
3.1	Aptos Creek. The trail is just to the left on the other side of the creek.
3.4	Trail climbs to Aptos Creek Road and ends. Turn around to ride back down.
4.0	Back to entrance booth.

Riding directly above Aptos Creek.

Vienna Woods Loop

The Vienna Woods Trail with Aptos Creek in the background.

Location: Aptos; near Cabrillo College.

Distance: 3.5 miles.

Elevation: 100/440 ft.

Trail Surface: 100% singletrack (sometime wide-ish).

Type of Ride: Loop (figure-8) with an out & back section.

Terrain: Dense redwood forest; creek crossings.

Technical Level: Medium; trail is often silky smooth, but look out for surprise downed trees and quick changes in elevation.
Exertion Level: Moderate; a gradual 1+ mile climb out.

Highlights: This little nature-emersing loop maximizes some of the best open singletrack within the maze-like lower Nisene trail network, and is a great way to connect with other trails in the area. The ride crosses Aptos Creek a few times, and passes plenty of mossy fern grottos and redwood trees. With everything from smooth bermed corners to more technical segments, this ride will delight any casual biker or nature lover. More type-A riders will want to combine trails for a longer ride. In the future, there may be an agreement to allow a public easement through nearby property, connecting Cabrillo College with the Vienna Woods Tr.

Options: Try riding in different directions and/or add a longer section by riding all of Aptos Rancho Trail or Aptos Creek Fire Road.

Note: There may or may not be bridges at the creek crossings! Crossing when the water levels are high could

Singletrack Splendor

cause a surprise swim, which is not recommended.

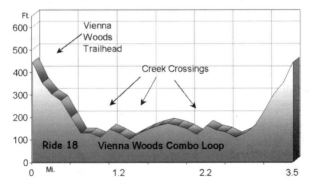

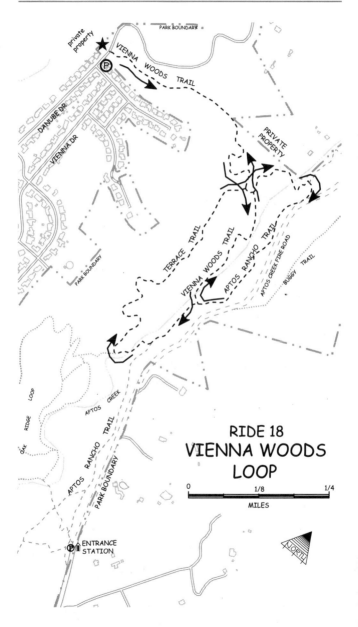

PARK BOUNDARY

private property

VIENNA WOODS TRAIL

DANUBE DR

VIENNA DR

PRIVATE PROPERTY

TERRACE TRAIL

VIENNA WOODS TRAIL

APTOS RANCHO TRAIL

APTOS CREEK FIRE ROAD

BUGGY TRAIL

OAK RIDGE LOOP

APTOS CREEK

APTOS RANCHO TRAIL

PARK BOUNDARY

RIDE 18
VIENNA WOODS
LOOP

0   1/8   1/4

MILES

ENTRANCE STATION

NORTH

Directions/Access: From Santa Cruz, take Highway 1 south to Park Ave exit and head inland. In about .4 miles, turn right onto Soquel Drive. After 1 mile, make a left and head up Vienna Drive. In just under a mile, turn left on Wilshire Drive and make a quick right on Danube Drive. Park on the right hand side in front of the "Stop: Private Road" sign. The trailhead is about 20 feet beyond the sign on the right.

Mileage Guide	
0.0	Vienna Woods Trail is on the right just up "Mesa Grande Rd."
.60	Major intersection! Keep going straight on Vienna Woods/Terrace Trail past the sign. About 200 feet ahead, make a sharp right onto the lower portion of Vienna Woods Trail. Ignore any spur trails off to the side.
.90	Creek crossing ahead. Ride up the bank on the other side, and turn right onto Aptos Rancho Tr. (Avoid at high flows).
1.1	Turn right onto posted Terrace Tr. and head for the creek again (or expand the ride by pedaling further on Aptos Rancho Trail).
1.2	After crossing the creek, watch out for stinging nettles!
1.3	When you come to the split in the trail, go right on Terrace Trail. (Its signed Terrace Connection.)
1.5	Stay straight; ignore spur trails that go down the bank.
1.7	Back to the major intersection again. Veer right and stay on Terrace Trail for a winding rollercoaster section of trail! (Pedal past the Vienna Woods Trail turnoff that is just ahead on the right).
1.9	Cross over the bridge and head leftwards up the bank toward Aptos Rancho Trail. (No bridge in the winter!)
2.0	Go right on Aptos Rancho Trail.
2.1	Giant tree-root ledge!
2.4	Make a sharp right on the unsigned Vienna Woods Trail and cross the creek for the last time.
2.7	Head left at the split. As you quickly come to the next intersection, keep going straight on Vienna Woods Trail.
3.3	Back at the trailhead.

Aptos Creek Fire Road:
To Sand Point Overlook

Aptos Creek Fire Road.

Location: Aptos; 6 miles southeast of Santa Cruz.

Distance: 17 miles roundtrip.

Elevation: 160/1600 ft.

Trail Surface: 100% dirt & fire road.

Type of Ride: Out & Back.

Terrain: Shady young redwood forest; Aptos and Bridge Creeks; excellent ocean and ridge views.

Technical Level: Easy; it's a fairly smooth and wide road for the most part. Small potholes develop with the winter rain.

Exertion Level: Strenuous. The first 3.8 miles are mellow, but the fire road steepens for the remaining 4.7 miles as it climbs up to the overlook.

Highlights: This out and back ride is one of the most highly utilized in all of Santa Cruz. Riding while thoroughly immersed in nature, this is one of the most rewarding workouts available. At Sand Point, you will be blessed with refreshing views of forested ridges descending into Monterey Bay (if its not foggy)!

Options: Any length ride is possible. Families may opt to ride the first 3 or so miles to one of the picnic areas. Rides can also be lengthened by riding beyond the overlook to Santa Rosalia Mountain (Ride 20), or riding a loop with Hinckley Basin Fire Road (Ride 21). To gain some singletrack, ride up Aptos Rancho Trail to the Steel Bridge (Ride 17).

Note: Mountain bikes are only allowed on the fire roads beyond the Steel Bridge. Tickets will be issued to those who ride any of the coveted singletrack trails back down, particularly on West Ridge Trail.

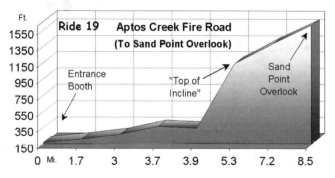

Directions/Access: From Santa Cruz, take Highway 1 south to State Park Dr. exit (# 435) in Aptos. Go inland (left) and take a right onto Soquel Drive. As you enter the Aptos Village area, make a left on Aptos Creek Road. You can park near the trailhead, just past the entrance booth ($6 self-pay). Or for a little longer ride, many people prefer to park behind the Aptos Station in town. The mileage guide for this ride begins just beyond the entrance booth where the pavement ends.

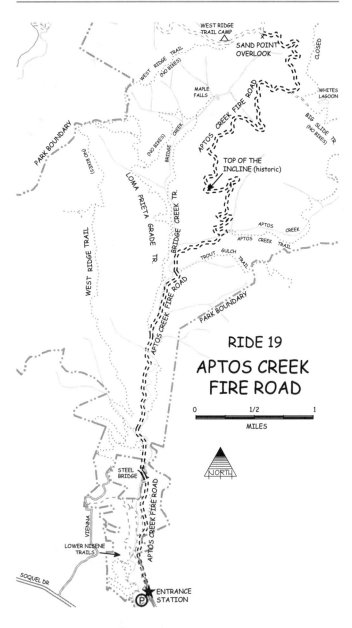

WEST RIDGE
TRAIL CAMP

SAND POINT
OVERLOOK

CLOSED

WEST RIDGE TRAIL
(NO BIKES)

APTOS CREEK FIRE ROAD

MAPLE
FALLS

WHITES
LAGOON

PARK BOUNDARY

(NO BIKES)

(NO BIKES)

BRIDGE CREEK

BIG SLIDE TR.
(NO BIKES)

TOP OF THE
INCLINE (historic)

LOMA PRIETA GRADE TR.

BRIDGE CREEK TR.

APTOS CREEK

APTOS CREEK TRAIL

WEST RIDGE TRAIL

APTOS CREEK FIRE ROAD

TROUT GULCH TRAIL

PARK BOUNDARY

RIDE 19
APTOS CREEK
FIRE ROAD

0   1/2   1

MILES

NORTH

STEEL
BRIDGE

VIENNA

APTOS CREEK FIRE ROAD

LOWER NISENE
TRAILS

SOQUEL DR

ENTRANCE
STATION

P

Crossing the wood-decked 'steel bridge' after biking to Sand Point.

Mileage Guide

0.0	Just beyond the entrance booth, the pavement on Aptos Creek Road gives way to packed dirt. The next 3.8 miles are a relatively easy ride.
1.1	Pass Aptos Rancho Trail and George's Picnic Area.
1.2	Cross over the Steel Bridge.
1.5	Roll on by West Ridge Trailhead off to the left.
2.2	The road splits at the Porter Family Picnic area. Just ahead on the left, the official Aptos Creek Fire Road begins at the gate.
2.8	The historic Loma Prieta Mill Site is on the left.
3.8	Stay to the left after the bridge crossing. Here, a panel describing the Loma Prieta Earthquake Epicenter marks the start of the incline. From now on, the fire road will provide more of an intense workout.
5.3	You've reached the "Top of Incline." Don't celebrate yet; this refers to the historic logging operation and is not the top of the climb. Although, the road wont be quite as steep since it starts to follow the old railroad grade again.

8.5	Sand Point Overlook! If it is clear, grandiose views await you! Monterey Bay frames Bridge Creek Canyon to the South, while the town of Santa Cruz appears in the southwest. Looking west across the Ben Lomond Ridge are views from UCSC to Big Basin. If you're eager for more elevation, continue on up to the right on upper Aptos Creek Fire Road (Ride 20). Another option is to take Hinckley Basin Fire Road (Ride 21), which is to your left. Passing West Ridge trail, it descends to Olive Springs Road and on to Old San Jose Road. However, most people opt to ride Aptos Creek Fire Road down as an out & back ride.
17	By this point you should finally be cooled down from the climb! After one long descent, you are back at the entrance booth.

Lonely bike and ocean views at Sand Point Overlook.

Upper Aptos Creek Fire Road:
Sand Point Overlook to Buzzard Lagoon Road

Cotton balls and oak trees on upper Aptos Creek Fire Road.

Location: In the center of The Forest of Nisene Marks.

Distance: 3.4 miles one-way to Santa Rosalia Ridge Overlook; 5.8 miles to Buzzard Lagoon Road.

Elevation: 1600/2600 ft.

Trail Surface: 100% fire road.

Type of Ride: Out & Back.

Terrain: Redwood forest; mountain ridge; viewpoint.

Technical Level: Easy; fairly smooth and wide road for the most part.

Exertion Level: Strenuous. By this point you've already had a pretty good warm up; to say the least.

Highlights: For endurance maniacs, there are many more miles to tackle beyond Sand Point Overlook. With far-reaching views and forest scenery, the ride takes you to one of the highest points in the county; Santa Rosalia Mountain on the edge of Soquel Demonstration Forest.

Options: Many riders simply bike to the Santa Rosalia Ridge Overlook (also known as Buzzard Lagoon Overview) as an out & back. Depending on where you rode in from, you can connect the ride with Hinckley Basin Fire Rd (Ride 21), Lower Aptos Creek Fire Rd (Ride 19), or Buzzard Lagoon Rd. Also, from the Santa Rosalia viewpoint, you can descend into Soquel Demonstration Forest via sweet singletrack (see Ride 22).

Note: Just another friendly reminder that bikes are officially allowed only on the dirt roads in this part of Nisene Marks.

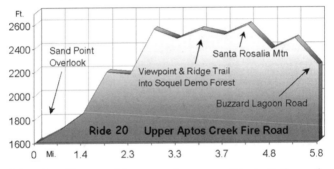

Directions/Access: Most people access this trail from the Nisene Marks main entrance in Aptos by riding up the lower section of Aptos Creek Fire Road. It can also be accessed from Hinckley Basin Fire Road commencing from Old San Jose Road, or from the opposite direction on Buzzard Lagoon Road in Corralitos, or from the Soquel Demonstration Forest.

Above the fog on Santa Rosalia Ridge.

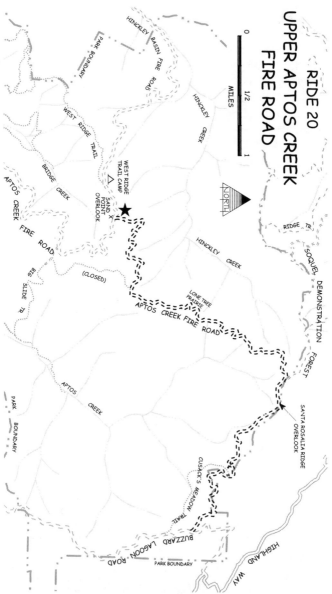

RIDE 20
UPPER APTOS CREEK
FIRE ROAD

Mileage Guide

0.0	Sand Point Overlook. After taking in this magnificent viewpoint, start riding up Aptos Creek Fire Road by staying to the right. Ignore any spur or pig trails veering off.
1.9	On the left is Lone Tree Prairie; historical logging site.
3.4	Santa Rosalia Ridge Overlook (Buzzard Lagoon Overview). Great place to take a break or turn around. There's a tree-framed viewpoint on the right, and the Ridge Trail (Soquel Demonstration Forest) is on the left. If you're burning for more, keep heading up Santa Rosalia Mountain.
4.2	Here, on Santa Rosalia Mountain, you are riding on some of the highest sections of trail in Santa Cruz. If this is not your final destination, you can keep exploring by riding down the fire road toward Buzzard Lagoon Road.
4.3	Aptos Creek Fire Road gate.
4.7	At the bottom of the trough on the right is Cusack's Meadow Trail, which ends on Buzzard Lagoon Road. Although some bikers utilize this trail, it is inside of Nisene Marks State Park and officially closed to bicycles.
5.8	Buzzard Lagoon Road. Turning left will point you in the direction of the lower Soquel Demonstration Forest entrance, via Highland Way. Turning right goes toward Buzzard Lagoon and the bottom of Cusack's Meadow Trail. And, of course, turning around takes you back the way you came.

A cloud burst viewed from the unmarked overlook off of upper Aptos Creek Fire Road.

Hinckley Basin Fire Road:
To Sand Point Overlook

Oxygen is abundant and free here.

Location: Soquel; 4 miles east of Santa Cruz.
Distance: 3.2 miles each way.
Elevation: 360/1600 ft.
Trail Surface: 100% dirt road.
Type of Ride: Out & Back; or a segment in a loop.
Terrain: Forest; creek crossings.
Technical Level: Easy; a mostly smooth and wide road.
Exertion Level: Very Strenuous.

Highlights: Rising quickly into the heart of Nisene Marks, Hinckley Basin Fire Road is a tough work out and not nearly as busy as Aptos Creek Fire Road. The route commences at the lush confluence of Soquel Creek and Hinckley Creek and climbs quickly to West Ridge Camp, Aptos Creek Fire Road, and Sand Point Overlook. At Sand Point, the forest opens up to showcase Monterey Bay and the city of Santa Cruz.

Options: For a longer ride, keep biking up Aptos Creek Fire Rd (Ride 20). Some people ride beyond the Overlook at Santa Rosalia Mountain, or make a loop with the lower section of Aptos Creek Rd (Ride 19), Soquel Dr, and Old San Jose Rd.

Note: There are creek crossings at the beginning of this ride that may not be passable after recent rain.

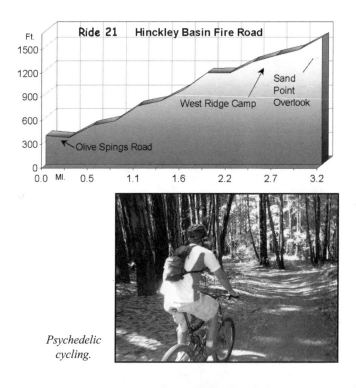

Psychedelic cycling.

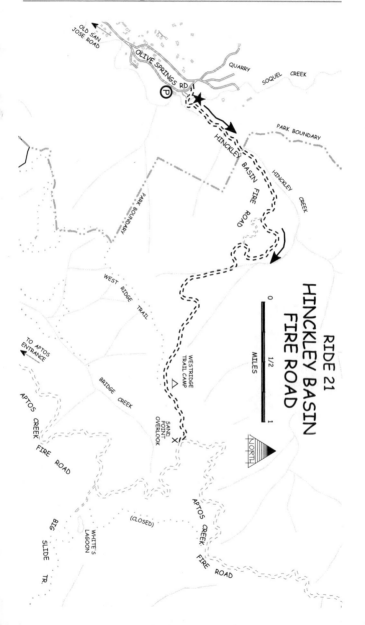

RIDE 21
HINCKLEY BASIN
FIRE ROAD

Directions/Access: Take Highway 1 south from Santa Cruz, and exit Bay/Porter St. Head inland and cross Soquel Dr. The street becomes Old San Jose Rd. After approximately 4.5 miles, turn right and drive up Olive Springs Road for about 1.3 miles. Parking is available on the right side of the road, before or after the quarry staging area. You'll spot a gated road across from the quarry weight station labeled "no trespassing" and "no parking." The gated dirt road for this ride is the next one up, on the right and across from the "exit" of the quarry staging area. This road is a public easement. Hinckley Basin Fire Rd is also accessed from Aptos Creek Fire Road (Ride 19).

Mileage Guide	
0.0	From Olive Springs Road, turn right and pass around the gate. The first .4 miles of the ride involves small creek crossings; be sure to spot the seasonal waterfall at the last crossing on the right.
1.2	As the road splits here; stay to the left. Ignore old logging roads and private home access roads veering off.
1.5	Again, stay left as you pedal by private property.
1.7	Cruise around the gate ahead.
2.7	West Ridge Camp & Trail. Keep on cranking up.
3.2	Payoff time! Sand Point Overlook! After taking in the sights, you can either ride on Aptos Creek Fire Road or head back down Hinckley Road.
6.4	Back at the Hinckley trailhead.

Flora framing fauna.

Epic Nisene-Demo Ride

Flow that will blow your mind and make you glow.

Location: Aptos, 6.5 miles southeast of Santa Cruz.
Distance: 33+ miles, depending on options chosen.
Elevation: 150/2550 ft.
Trail Surface: 20% singletrack; 80% fire roads; more single-track options possible.
Type of Ride: Out & back with loop.
Terrain: Dense forest; creeks; ridges; mountains; great views.
Technical Level: Ranges from Easy to Very Difficult.
Exertion Level: Very Strenuous; extreme mega work out.

Highlights: Riding from the coast to the 'summit' and back, this is a dream workout of epic proportions for the serious cross-country mountain biker. With gut-wrenching uphills and kamikaze downhills, there is an endless variety of beautiful terrain and plenty of challenge as you ride the length of both Nisene Marks and Soquel Demonstration forest!

Options: You can alternate some of the fire road sections for more singletrack, such as in the lower Nisene Marks area.

Note: Bring lots of food and water.

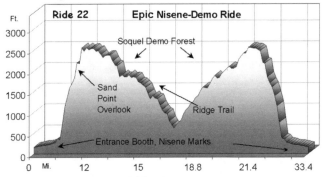

Directions/Access: See Ride 19.

Mileage Guide	
0.0	At the entrance booth, ride up Aptos Creek Road.
1.2	Steel bridge.
8.5	Sand Point Overlook! Spectacular place to catch your breath. When you're ready to endure more, stay to the right on Aptos Creek Fire Road and keep charging up!
11.9	Intersection at the Santa Rosalia Overlook (Buzzard Lagoon Overview). Go left at the sign to ride Soquel Demo Forest's Ridge Trail! As you descend this ripping trail, there will be 5 options to turn right and descend to Hihn Mill Road. The farther you go, the longer the loop! For detailed information on these trails see Rides 25 A-G
12.5	Corral Trail is a nice descent on the right (see Ride 25B).
13.5	Continuing on Ridge Trail, you will pass a helipad on the right. Just ahead is the second option; Sulphur Springs Trail (Ride 25C), a nice way to climb back up on the return. Stay left to keep riding Ridge Trail.

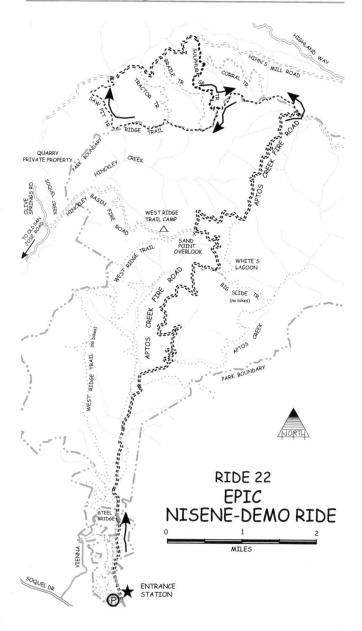

RIDE 22
EPIC
NISENE-DEMO RIDE

14.0	Braille Trail (see 25D) is on the right.
14.5	Tractor Trail (see 25E) is next up.
15.4	After a quick climb, veer right to descend Saw Pit Trail (25F).
16.7	After a great downhill section, turn right on Hihn Mill Road to start a gradual climb out.
17.3	On the right, you'll pass the bottom of Tractor Trail, which is one option for a nice gradual climb back up.
17.7	If you stayed on Hihn Mill, keep chugging by Braille Trail.
18.6	Finally you'll come to Sulphur Springs Trail (dirt road). Turn right and start cranking all the way to the top.
20.1	Ridge Trail! Turn left and pedal back into Nisene Marks. The remainder of the ride is an out & back.
21.7	Turn right on Aptos Creek Fire Road.
25.1	Sand Point Overlook.
32.4	Steel Bridge.
33.6	Entrance Booth. How does a super-burrito sound?

A 1,000 words still wouldn't describe what this picture tells.

Soquel Demonstration State Forest

Demonstrating Disneyland style features.

Providing some of Santa Cruz's most challenging terrain, Soquel Demonstration State Forest offers almost 21 miles of mountain biking trails. Of these trails, 10+ miles are excellent singletrack with plenty of fun-sized bike stunts; log rides, see -saws, jumps, and jibs! Nestled between the Forest of Nisene Marks and upper Soquel Creek, the "Demo Forest's" topography is very steep. However, the exhilarating singletrack descents are well worth the grinding uphill sections. Recent flow-improving reroutes and trail work will certainly leave your cheeks hurting from the grin factor.

Operated by the California Department of Forestry and Fire Protection, Soquel Demonstration Forest is used for forest management projects as well as recreation. It has no facilities, bathrooms, or formal parking (i.e. you have to pee in the bushes). The main access area is located 6 miles east of Soquel-San Jose Road (Old San Jose Road) on Highland Way.

Outer Demo Loop

Can't see the forest for the trail.

Location: Bordering the northern boundary of Nisene Marks State Park, near the "Summit."

Distance: 12-15 miles.

Elevation: 1600/2600 ft.

Trail Surface: 40% singletrack; 60% dirt/fire/paved roads.

Type of Ride: Loop.

Terrain: Forest; mountain ridge; steep terrain; views.
Technical Level: Difficult/Very Difficult; steep downhill trails with optional stunts.
Exertion Level: Strenuous.

Highlights: This Santa Cruz classic is a must-do ride! As one of the more challenging loops in Santa Cruz, you'll experience endorphin rushes from the invigorating climbs and pure downhill bliss on insane singletrack with optional freeride stunts. Don't forget to catch an occasional glimpse of the ocean vistas.

Options: You can wimp out or step-it-up by choosing which stunts to hit and what trail to descend. See specific trail descriptions; Rides 25 A-F. For the ultimate ride, add an "Inner Demo Loop" (Ride 24) to the ride.

Note: This ride describes the longest possible loop; the full length of Ridge Trail to Saw Pit Trail. Keep in mind that most of the final jaunt on Hihn's Mill is uphill; the farther you ride down on the Ridge Trail, the farther you will have to climb out....it is way worth it though!

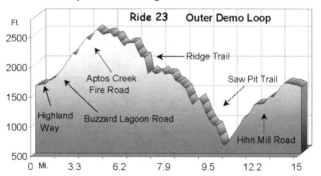

Directions/Access: From Santa Cruz or San Jose, take Highway 17 to the "Summit." Exit and head east on Summit Rd (from Santa Cruz, this will be on the right). You will be on this road for about 10 miles. When the road forks, stay on Highland Way; (after the stop sign, you will veer right, and at the next split stay left). As the road descends into the canyon, look on the right for the dirt pull-out and a small green sign that says "Soquel Demonstration State Forest." You'll see a bridge with bright yellow railing over the creek. Park here or drive across the bridge and park in the dirt pullout area on the right.   (Don't leave valuables in your car here!) Soquel Demonstration Forest can also be reached by taking Soquel-San Jose Rd (Old San Jose Rd) from Soquel; turn right on Highland Way and drive 6 miles southeast.

A little playground for the not-so-blind on the Braille Trail.

Mileage Guide	
0.0	From the dirt parking area by the yellow bridge, ride east (up the canyon) on Highland Way.
2.0	At the top, turn right on Buzzard Lagoon Road (dirt).
2.5	Buzzard Lagoon Road makes a sharp left turn here. Just ahead, you will enter the Forest of Nisene Marks beyond the gate.
3.0	At the road split, turn right onto the fire road and keep cranking. This becomes Aptos Creek Fire Road. (You may see bikers continue riding on Buzzard Lagoon Road to Cusack's Meadow Trail for more singletrack. However, it is officially off limits for bikes.)
3.8	Ignore the private maintenance road/trail on the right. How about a little downhill relief now!?

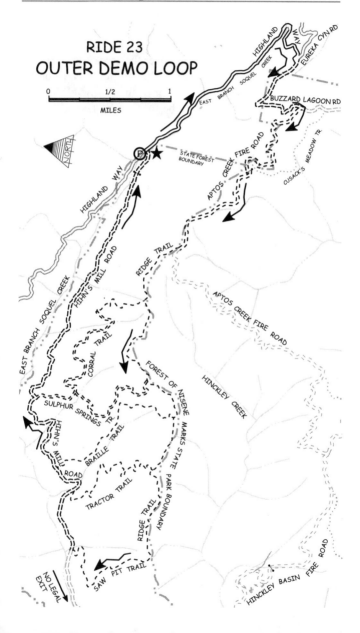

RIDE 23
OUTER DEMO LOOP

0   1/2   1
MILES

NORTH

HIGHLAND WAY

EAST BRANCH SOQUEL CREEK

EUREKA CYN RD

BUZZARD LAGOON RD

CUSACK'S MEADOW TR

STATE FOREST BOUNDARY

APTOS CREEK FIRE ROAD

HIGHLAND WAY

HIHN'S MILL ROAD

RIDGE TRAIL

CORRAL TRAIL

SULPHUR SPRINGS TR

BRAILLE TRAIL

HIHN'S MILL ROAD

TRACTOR TRAIL

RIDGE TRAIL

FOREST OF NISENE MARKS STATE PARK BOUNDARY

APTOS CREEK FIRE ROAD

HINCKLEY CREEK

SAW PIT TRAIL

NO LEGAL EXIT

HINCKLEY BASIN FIRE ROAD

4.0	At the bottom of the trough, you will pass the top of Cusack's Meadow Trail (no bikes). Continue up the fire road.
4.3	Pass around the Nisene Marks gate.
5.3	At the green sign, the Ridge Trail descends on the right. Before dropping in to Soquel Demo Forest, you can revitalize your soul by taking in the open vista of the bay. As you head down Ridge Trail, there will progressively be five options to turn right and descend back to Hihn's Mill Road which will ultimately take you to your car. (See Rides 25 A-F for details on specific trails).
5.9	Corral Trail is on the right (see 25B).
6.8	Continuing on Ridge Trail, you will pass by a helipad off to the right. Just ahead Sulphur Springs Trail (dirt road, see 25C). Stay left and keep riding Ridge Trail.
7.3	Braille Trail (See 25D) is on the right.
7.8	Tractor Trail (see 25E) is next up. If you keep riding left beyond on Ridge, the next section will include some steep and technical sections of trail.
8.8	This is the end of the Ridge Trail. Your last option is to turn right on Saw Pit Trail (see 25F).
10.0	After that permagrin-inducing downhill, turn right on Hihn's Mill Road to start a long climb back.
10.6	On the right, you'll pass the bottom of Tractor Trail.
11.0	Keep chugging by Braille Trail.
11.9	Next you'll pass Sulphur Springs Trailhead.
14.9	Yellow gate.
15.0	Cross yellow-railed bridge to your car.

Unless they paint it, the yellow railed bridge marks the entrance to the park.

Inner Demo Loop

One should try this at home first.

Location: North of Nisene Marks near the "Summit."
Distance: 12-13.5 miles.
Elevation: 1600/2600 ft.
Trail Surface: 50% singletrack; 50% fire road (variable).
Type of Ride: Loop.
Terrain: Dense forest; steep mountain riding, logs, jumps, drops, intermediate to advanced level stunts.
Technical Level: Difficult/Most Difficult; depends on trail choice.
Exertion Level: Strenuous/Very Strenuous.

Highlights: This is an intense ride with steep heart-thumping uphills and will-testing stunt laden downhills. The "Demo Forest" contains some of the only legal intermediate freeriding in California. With a plethora of options to keep you stoked, many hardcore riders will do multiple loops! Ride up Sulphur Springs Trail, and then descend down Corral Trail or Ridge Trail to Braille, Tractor, or Saw Pit Trails.

Options: You can affect the difficulty of the ride by choosing which trail to descend or ascend. See Rides 25 A-F. One popular option is to ride a double loop by climbing Sulphur Springs and later Tractor Trail, and descending Corral, Braille, and/or Sawpit Trails.

Note: Only attempt the stunts if your experience matches the level of difficulty.

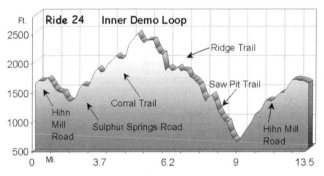

Directions/Access: See Ride 23.

Ride the wind, ghost rider.

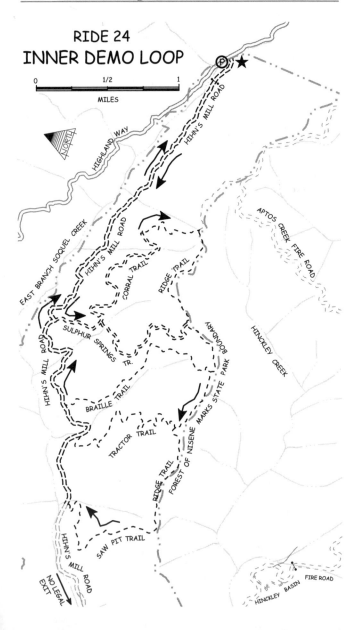

RIDE 24
INNER DEMO LOOP

0   1/2   1
MILES

NORTH

HIGHLAND WAY

HIHN'S MILL ROAD

EAST BRANCH SOQUEL CREEK

HIHN'S MILL ROAD

CORRAL TRAIL

RIDGE TRAIL

APTOS CREEK FIRE ROAD

SULPHUR SPRINGS TR.

BOUNDARY

HINCKLEY CREEK

HIHN'S MILL ROAD

BRAILLE TRAIL

TRACTOR TRAIL

FOREST OF NISENE MARKS STATE PARK

RIDGE TRAIL

SAW PIT TRAIL

HIHN'S MILL ROAD

NO LEGAL EXIT

HINCKLEY BASIN

FIRE ROAD

Mileage Guide	
0.0	From the Highland Way parking area, cross the yellow-railed bridge and head up Hihn's Mill Road.
.20	Pedal past the gate and the information panel.
2.5	Turn left at Sulphur Springs Trail (dirt road).
2.7	Keep going straight; a road will merge on the right.
2.9	Corral Trail splits off Sulphur Springs to the left (straight). Both ways have very steep sections as they ascend to the ridge trail. To maximize singletrack riding, take Corral Trail. (Or take Sulphur Springs all the way up for a steep dirt road climb.)
4.7	Ridge Trail. You can breathe now! Turn right and start your descent. (There are some short uphill sections). As you ride Ridge Trail, there are four trail choices to turn right on.
5.6	Pass by the helipad on the right. Just ahead is Sulphur Springs Tr (see 25C). Stay left and keep riding Ridge Tr.
6.1	The world-famous Braille Trail (see 25D) is on the right.
6.5	Tractor Trail, the easiest trail with the least stunts (see 25E), is next up. Beyond this point, Ridge Trail has some steep and technical downhill sections with log rides and small jumps scattered throughout.
7.5	If your cheeks hurt from smiling too much, you can give them a break as you grunt up this next very steep section. This will take you to the end of the Ridge Trail. Turn right to bomb Saw Pit Trail (see 25F).
8.8	Go right on Hihn's Mill Road for a long gradual climb back.
9.5	Pass by Tractor Trail.
9.8	Next you'll pass by Braille Trail.
10.7	Keep cranking by Sulphur Springs Trailhead.
13.5	Cross yellow-railed bridge and head back to your car.

The Demo Forest Trail Guide

25A. Ridge Trail

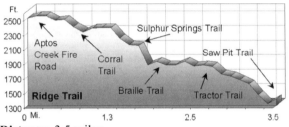

Distance: 3.5 miles.

Sections: .65 mi. from Ridge Trailhead to Corral; .95 mi. from Corral to Sulphur Springs; .5 mi. from Sulphur Springs to Braille; .5 mi. from Braille to Tractor; .9 mi. from Tractor to Saw Pit.

Elevation: 1320/2520 ft.

Trail Surface: 100% singletrack.

Technical Level: Ranges from Medium to Most Difficult.

Exertion Level: Moderate. If you happen to ride this uphill, it rates Strenuous/Very Strenuous.

Highlights: One of the most fun sections of downhill in the county! Laced with intermediate freeride stunts, the trail is fast, challenging, sometimes very technical. Don't miss some of the sweeping forest and ocean views!

Signature Demo Forest singletrack.

The following trails 25 B-F descend perpendicularly from Ridge Trail to Hihn's Mill Road:

25B. Corral Trail

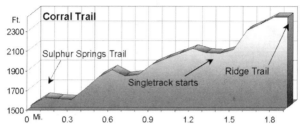

Distance: 1.8 miles.
Distance from Ridge Trailhead to top of Trail: .65 miles.
Distance from Sulphur Springs Trail bottom on Hihn's Mill Rd to entrance parking: 2.5 miles.
Elevation: 1520/2420 ft.

Trail Surface: 35% singletrack; 65% fire road-turning-to-trail.
Technical Level: Difficult; optional stunts throughout.
Exertion Level: Moderate. Very Strenuous when climbing.
Highlights: This trail has become a popular descent with several fun log rides, drops, banked turns, and wall-jibs.

Log Ride on Corral Trail.

25C. Sulphur Springs Trail

Distance: 1.5 miles.
Distance from Ridge Trailhead to top of Trail: 1.6 miles.
Distance from Trail bottom on Hihn's Mill Rd to entrance parking: 2.5 miles.
Elevation: 1350 /2200 ft.
Trail Surface: 100% dirt road.

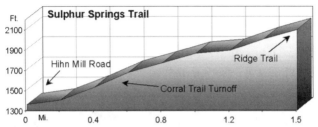

Technical Level: Moderate; mostly smooth but very steep.
Exertion Level: Very Strenuous climbing uphill.

Highlights: This road is most commonly used to climb up to access Ridge Trail due to its less technical dirt road nature.

25D. Braille Trail

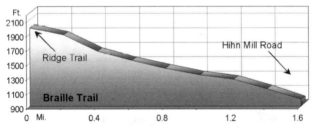

Distance: 1.6 miles.

Distance from Ridge Trailhead to top of Trail: 2.1 miles.

Distance from Trail bottom on Hihn's Mill Rd to entrance parking: 3.4 miles.

Elevation: 1000/1990 ft.
Trail Surface: 100% singletrack.
Technical Level: Most Difficult; a few very steep sections with some free-riding obstacles, although it is easy to ride around and avoid them.
Exertion Level: Moderate.
Historic Braille Trail stunt.

Highlights: What used to be one of the best kept secrets in Santa Cruz, is now one of the best "downhill" trails in the county! Full of steep chutes, jumps, logs, seesaws, banked turns, and vertical drops, this fast trail is a skill-testing downhill park.

25E. Tractor Trail

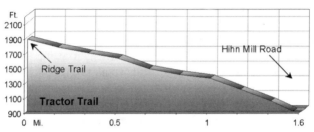

Distance: 1.6 miles.
Distance from Ridge Trailhead to top of Trail: 2.6 miles.
Distance from Trail bottom on Hihn's Mill Rd to entrance parking: 3.9 miles.
Elevation: 850/1870 ft.
Trail Surface: 100% singletrack.
Technical Level: Difficult/Medium; some very steep sections.
Exertion Level: Strenuous but gradual when ascending.
Highlights: With smooth groovy turns, fast straight-aways, and a few jumps, the gradual nature of the trail is ideal for an easy descent or for climbing back up for a second loop.

25F. Saw Pit Trail

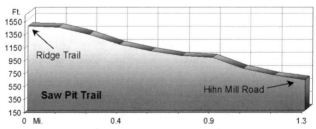

Distance: 1.25 miles.

Distance from Ridge Trailhead to top of Trail: 3.5 miles.
Distance from Trail bottom on Hihn's Mill Rd to entrance parking: 4.5 miles.
Elevation: 620/1400 ft.
Trail Surface: 100% singletrack.
Technical level: Most Difficult; steep sections.
Exertion Level: Moderate/Strenuous when riding uphill.
Highlights: Another insane redwood forest trail with some fun size hip jumps and a few drops along a windy and groovy trail. Riding this trail involves riding the full length of the Ridge Trail and thus maximizes the most downhill singletrack in the park. Along with the preceding Ridge Trail, it also provides the most stunts. Don't forget that it drops you way down Hihn's Mill road with a relatively long ride back to the entrance.

25G.   Hihn's Mill Road

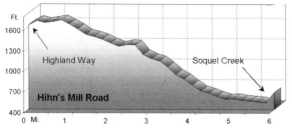

Distance: 6 miles one-way; 5 miles to Badger Springs.
Elevation: 480/1690 ft.
Trail Surface: 100% dirt road.
Technical Level: Easy.
Exertion Level: Strenuous.
Highlights: Paralleling Soquel Creek, this road is most often used to access the singletrack trails. It is also a good out & back workout ride away from the crowds. Hihn's Mill passes Badger Springs picnic area, accesses Long Ridge Road and Amaya Creek Road, and has a bridge crossing over Soquel Creek. Unfortunately, there is no public access through adjoining properties.

25H. Amaya Road

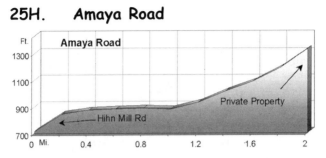

Distance: 2 miles one-way; ends at private property.
Elevation: 500/1250 ft.
Trail Surface: 100% dirt road.
Technical Level: Easy.
Exertion Level: Strenuous.
Highlights: If you are die-hard and want to add a few more uphill miles to Hihn's Mill Road, this is for you.

25I. Long Ridge Road

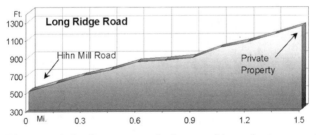

Distance: 1.5 miles one-way, before reaching private property.
Elevation: 510/1250 ft.
Trail Surface: 100% dirt road.
Technical Level: Easy.
Exertion Level: Strenuous.
Highlights: Accessed from Hihn's Mill Road just after Badger Springs, this road tacks cross-country style mileage onto the lists of bike trails.

Big Basin Redwoods State Park

*Berry Creek Falls is a short hike off the
Waddell Creek/Skyline To The Sea Trail.*

Created in 1902, Big Basin is California's oldest State Park. It consists of over 18,000 acres of redwood, conifer, oak, and chaparral, and contains the largest forest of "ancient coast" redwoods south of San Francisco. As the park ranges from sea level to mountains over 2,000 feet high, the terrain varies from lush canyon bottoms to sparse chaparral-covered slopes. Most of the Waddell Creek watershed, which was formed by seismic uplift and subsequent erosion, is located within the boundaries of the park. Enhancing this coastal mountain scenery, are several creeks and waterfalls. One of the most dramatic falls is a short hike off the Waddell Creek bike ride.

Even though Big Basin contains over 80 miles of trails, only the fire roads are open to mountain bikes. These multi-use roads, however, cover an immense amount of turf, making for some excellent biking!

Multimedia information are available at the small museum and visitor center. Several campgrounds, including bike assessable trail camps, are located throughout the park. Dogs are not allowed on any trails.

The main park area is 22 miles northwest of Santa Cruz via Highways 9 and 236. The Waddell Creek/Skyline to the Sea Trail is located 13 miles northwest of Santa Cruz on Highway 1.

A pristine, secluded beach visible on the way up to
Waddell Creek and Big Basin State Park.

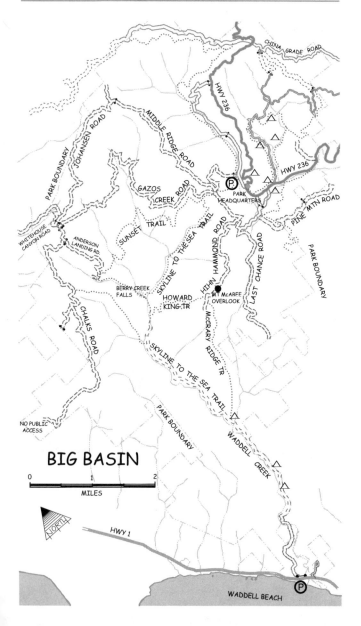

CHINA GRADE ROAD

HWY 236

HWY 236

PINE MTN ROAD

PARK BOUNDARY

PARK BOUNDARY

JOHANSEN ROAD

MIDDLE RIDGE ROAD

GAZOS CREEK ROAD

SUNSET TRAIL

SKYLINE TO THE SEA TRAIL

HIHN HAMMOND ROAD

LAST CHANCE ROAD

WHITEHOUSE CANYON ROAD

ANDERSON LANDING RD.

BERRY CREEK FALLS

HOWARD KING TR.

MT McABEE OVERLOOK

McCRARY RIDGE TR.

CHALKS ROAD

SKYLINE TO THE SEA TRAIL

NO PUBLIC ACCESS

WADDELL CREEK

BIG BASIN

0   1   2

MILES

NORTH

HWY 1

WADDELL BEACH

PARK HEADQUARTERS

PARK BOUNDARY

Waddell Creek Trail
(Skyline To The Sea Trail)

Where the biking ends and the hike to Berry Creek Falls begins.

Location: 13 miles north of Santa Cruz on Highway 1.

Distance: 11.8 miles.

Elevation: 20/320 ft.

Trail Surface: Primarily narrow fire road (it has naturally eroded into singletrack in some sections).

Type of Ride: Out & Back.

Terrain: Beach; forest; creeks; waterfall.

Technical Level: Easy; smooth surface with some more moderate sections where the road has become more of a trail.

Exertion Level: Mild; very gradual climb.

Highlights: Waddell Creek Trail is a fun cross country ride and multi-sport adventure for most ability levels. Starting at Waddell Beach, the ride begins in the open sun before cruising along fern-lined Waddell Creek in the moist lush redwood forest. At the end of the ride, there is a ¾ mile hike up to one of Santa Cruz's most fabulous waterfalls! A large bike rack accompanies the trailhead; don't forget your bike lock!

Options: Don't miss the Berry Creek Falls hike at the top of the bike ride. Gazos Creek Road is another out and back ride nearby (see Ride 28A).

Note: Biking is only allowed on fire roads in Big Basin.

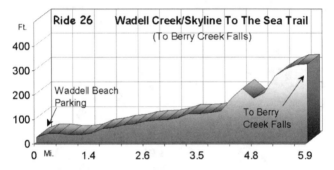

Ride 26   Waddell Creek/Skyline To The Sea Trail
(To Berry Creek Falls)

Waddell Beach Parking

To Berry Creek Falls

Directions/Access: From Santa Cruz, take Highway 1 North. After passing Western Drive, the last stoplight in Santa Cruz, it is about 9 ½ miles to Waddell Creek. After crossing over the creek, park at the beach parking on either side. A sign labeled "Big Basin State Park" confirms your location. The trailhead is on the inland side of Highway 1 opposite the Waddell Beach parking lot. Start at the gated paved entrance road.

To the delight of mountain bikers, the original fire road is turning into singletrack just above the creek.

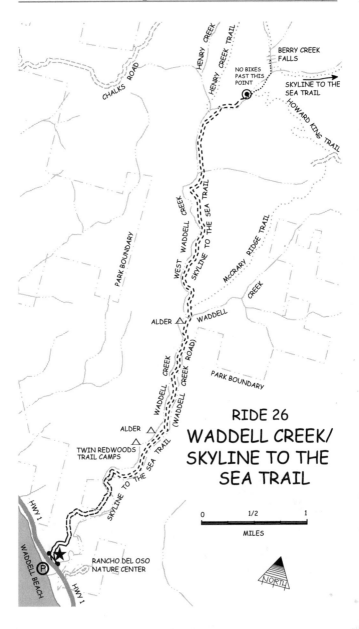

RIDE 26
WADDELL CREEK/
SKYLINE TO THE
SEA TRAIL

Mileage Guide

0.0	On the paved entrance road, ride around the gate and the information panel. There is a sign labeled "Skyline to the Sea Trail."
.40	Stay on the main road after passing the ranger station. After you ride around another gate, the road will become dirt.
.65	Ignore the road merging on the right.
1.1	Cross the bridge and pass by the private property.
1.7	Soon you'll ride by a couple trail camps in the redwoods.
3.0	This next section has some steeper singletrack switchbacks; the most technical portion of the ride.
3.2	Pass another trail camp.
3.3	Turn right on the trail just before you get to the Waddell Creek crossing. This will take you onto the bridge and back to the main trail.
4.9	Bridge crossing.
5.5	Stay to the right on the main road.
5.7	Another bridge crossing.
5.9	End of the line for bikes! Park your bike in the bike racks and prepare for a little hike to a big waterfall! The trail is just to the right of the information panel and crosses the creek on a small footbridge.
11.8	Back at Waddell parking lot.

Waddell Beach; a premiere kitesurfing spot near the trailhead.

Big Basin Loop

A redwood scene from a bikers point of view on the Big Basin loop.

Location: 25 miles northwest of Santa Cruz.

Distance: 13.2 miles; more with spur options.

Elevation: 880/2030 ft.

Trail Surface: 94% fire road; 6% paved road.

Type of Ride: Loop.

Terrain: Redwood forest; lots of small creeks; views!

Technical Level: Medium; some steep sections with occasional ruts and bumpy sandstone rocks.

Exertion Level: Very Strenuous; this rating is based upon the first few miles which have some very steep heart-pounding segments. The climb out is far more gradual.

Highlights: Not only is this a great workout with incredible scenery, it has plenty of remote, fast and furious downhill sections. Majestic mountain and ocean views, an abundance of creeks, and plenty of magnificent redwoods will stoke you the whole way!

Options: There are several other out & back spur roads to explore as well.

Note: Biking is not allowed on any singletrack trails.

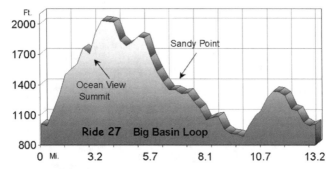

Directions/Access: From Santa Cruz, take Highway 9 (at the intersection of River St and Highway 1) 13 miles into Boulder Creek. Turn left on Highway 263 and take it for 9 miles to the park headquarters. Park in the lot across from the headquarters; (there is a small day-use fee).

Mileage Guide	
0.0	From the parking booth, ride north through the parking lot and pass the snack bar and nature lodge.
.30	Go left over the wood bridge and keep straight.
.40	Pedal around the brown gate as you ride up the canyon on Gazos Creek Road.
.50	The road now becomes dirt!
1.3	Go right on Middle Ridge Road and mentally prepare for some very steep sections ahead.
2.4	If you're starting to feel more sun and see open vistas, you are probably near Ocean View Summit! Great place to take a break before cranking on.
3.5	More great views from the ridge.
3.7	Gate.

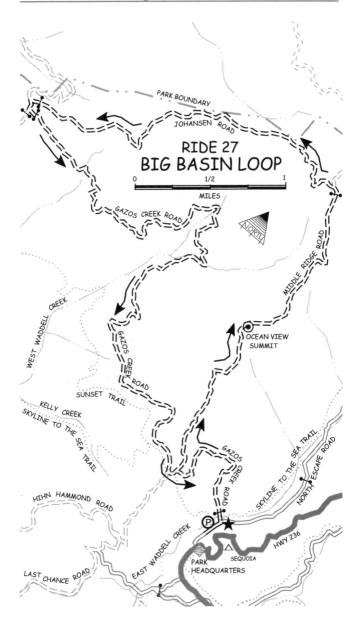

3.8	Go left at the intersection onto Johansen Road.
4.2	There will be more great views from the ridge.
4.4	Gate.
6.6	Pass around the big gate and go left on Gazos Creek Road. Soon, take another left and ride around yet another gate as you continue on Gazos Creek Road.
7.2	Spectacular ridge, mountain, and ocean views here!
8.8	Lots of small creeks in this area; look out for waterfalls in the rainy season.
9.7	Gate.
10.3	The next mile and a half will be a long but gradual uphill.
11.7	Downhill for the rest of the ride now!
11.9	Stay on the main road as you pass by other spur roads.
12.9	Turn right after crossing over the wood bridge.
13.2	End of the ride.

Gazos Creek Road has a few sections of Moab-like slickrock in dense redwood forests with ocean views to boot!

Big Basin Trail Guide

28A.   Gazos Creek Road

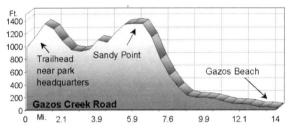

Distance: 14 miles.

Elevation: 20/1350 ft.

Trail Surface: 62 % dirt road; 38 % paved road.

Terrain: Dense forest; lots of creeks; some views; various strange bright orange sulphur-smelling springs.

Technical Level: Easy.

Exertion Level: Moderate/Strenuous.

Highlights: Gazos Creek Road cruises from the park headquarters all the way to Gazos beach. Some people ride the road as a one-way shuttle or as an out 'n' back from the beach.

28B.   Middle Ridge Road

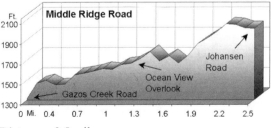

Distance: 2.5 miles.

Elevation: 1314/2050 ft.
Trail Surface: 100% dirt road.
Terrain: Forest; mountain ridge; ocean views.
Technical Level: Medium; some rocky sections.
Exertion Level: Very Strenuous; riding uphill.
Highlights: Connecting Gazos Creek and Johansen Roads, Middle Ridge Road has some fun and challenging sections. "Ocean View Summit" is about half way up.

28C. Hihn Hammond Road

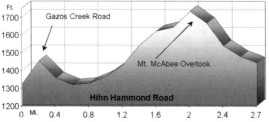

Distance: 2.7 miles; 2 miles to the overlook.
Elevation: 1310/1730 ft.
Trail Surface: 100% dirt road.
Terrain: Forest; overlook.
Technical Level: Medium.
Exertion Level: Moderate.
Highlights: At 2 miles, the Mt McAbee Overlook provides great views.

28D. Last Chance Road

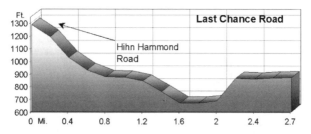

Distance: 2.7 miles.
Elevation: 660/1290 ft.
Trail Surface: 100% dirt road.
Terrain: Forest; creek crossing.
Technical Level: Moderate.
Exertion Level: Strenuous.
Highlights: This road winds along East Waddell Creek.

28E. Johansen Road

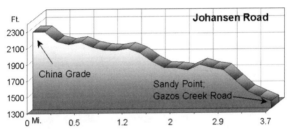

Distance: 3.7 miles.
Elevation: 1380/2250 ft.
Trail Surface: 100% dirt road.
Terrain: Dense forest; mountain views.
Technical Level: Easy.
Exertion Level: Very Strenuous if you ride uphill.
Highlights: Dropping from the north end of the park to Gazos Creek Road, Johansen Road contains one long fun downhill section when riding south.

28F. Whitehouse Canyon Road

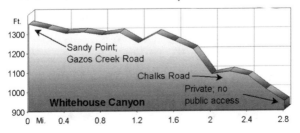

Distance: 2.8 miles.
Elevation: 950/1350 ft.
Trail Surface: 100% dirt road.
Terrain: Forest.
Technical Level: Medium.
Exertion Level: Moderate.
Highlights: There is also a 2.4-mile bottom section with public acce
off Highway 1, just south of Rossi Road. This takes you to an "unmai
tained" double track and a hiking trail to a viewpoint.

28G. Anderson Landing Road

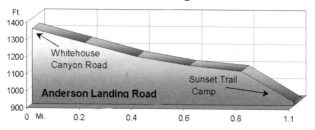

Distance: 1.1 miles one-way.
Elevation: 920/1340 ft.
Trail Surface: 100% dirt road.
Terrain: Dense forest; ridge; view area.
Technical Level: Easy.
Exertion Level: Moderate.
Highlights: Anderson Landing Road spurs off Whitehouse
Canyon Road and heads down to Sunset Trail Camp.

28H. Chalks Road

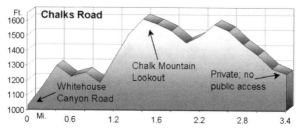

Distance: 3.4 miles; 1.5 miles to Chalk Mountain.
Elevation: 1030/1610 ft.
Trail Surface: 100% dirt road.
Terrain: Forest; viewpoint.
Technical Level: Medium.
Exertion Level: Strenuous.
Highlights: This road heads up to Chalk Mountain; a spectacular lookout just above "The Chalks." Here, Westridge hiking trail descends toward Waddell Beach.

Crossing Waddell Creek on a bridge to somewhere.

Saratoga Gap/Long Ridge Open Space Preserves

Is it the trail or the ocean views that are so breathtaking?

Located on the northern boundary of Santa Cruz County, Saratoga Gap and Long Ridge Open Space Preserves are filled with gorgeous scenery and great mountain biking. Meandering through forest and ocean-framed grasslands, the riding is a fun mix-mash of trails and fire roads. Due to the amount of singletrack, amazing views, and proximity to the San Jose area, the open space preserves are very popular and can be rather crowded on weekends. However, these bike parks are definitely worth the trip!

In addition to the rides featured in this book, mountain bikers can enjoy many more miles of riding beyond Long Ridge and Saratoga Gap. These open spaces are linked to Upper Stevens Creek County Park, Skyline Ridge Open Space Preserve, and a series of other parks in the south Skyline region. The trail-head is on the northeast quadrant of the junction of Highway 9 and Skyline Blvd (Highway 35). There are no bathrooms or water available. Trails are open from 8 am until sunset. Leashed dogs are permitted on designated trails only.

Saratoga Gap Trail

Singletrack like this is not only in a mountain biker's dreams.

Location: At the junction of Highway 9 and Skyline Blvd.
Distance: 4.4 miles.
Elevation: 2490/2690 ft.
Trail Surface: 100% singletrack.
Type of Ride: Out & Back.
Terrain: Shady forest with a section through grasslands.
Technical Level: Easy/Medium; trail is mostly smooth with various rocks and roots; some quick ups and downs.
Exertion Level: Moderate; short gradual climbs/descents.

Highlights: If you want a short ride with snappy elevation changes on high quality singletrack; look no further. Big ride

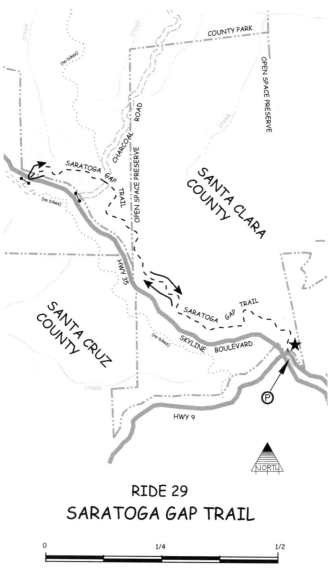

RIDE 29
SARATOGA GAP TRAIL

seekers may want to continue riding on the Bay Area Ridge Trail, but the Saratoga Gap Trail is a great out & back ride for mountain bike newbies or a quick after-work pedal.

Options: It is possible to keep riding as far as you want. See Ride 30 for more thrills.

Note: This is a high-use trail; don't forget to smile and wink.

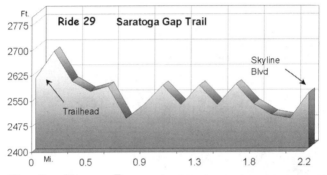

Directions/Access: From Santa Cruz, take Highway 9 all the way to Skyline Blvd (Highway 35) on the border of Santa Clara County. The trailhead is on the northeast side of the intersection. Parking is available directly in front of the trailhead or in the adjacent parking lot.

Trail Euphoria.

Mileage Guide	
0.0	Start riding up from the Saratoga Gap Trailhead.
1.8	Take the trail to the left as you reach the intersection area.
2.2	Skyline Blvd. The trail continues on the other side if you want to keep riding (Ride 30). Otherwise, ride back.
4.4	Back at the trailhead.

Long Ridge Loop

Revitalizing the soul in Long Ridge Open Space Preserve.

Location: The junction of Highway 9 and Skyline Blvd.
Distance: 10.7 miles; more possible.
Elevation: 2160/2670 ft.
Trail Surface: 66% singletrack; 34% fire road.
Type of Ride: Loop with an out & back section.
Terrain: Ocean views; grassy hills; forest; creek.
Technical Level: Medium.
Exertion Level: Moderate.

Highlights: One minute you'll be gliding through a lush oak, fir, and madrone forest; then suddenly you find yourself gazing over pristine hills of grass bounded by Santa Cruz county and the Pacific Ocean. On a clear day, the ocean vistas are simply incredible and all seen while pedaling an intermingled network of curvy smooth singletrack and pleasant fire roads.

Options: Many more miles can be tacked on by riding the Bay Area Ridge Trail beyond the Long Ridge/Peter's Creek intersection. Some people also do a larger and much steeper loop with Grizzly Flat Trail and Charcoal Road. This is only recommended if you love fast downhill descents followed by a relentless uphill section.

Note: Nice weekends attract lots of people to the trails; Ride accordingly.

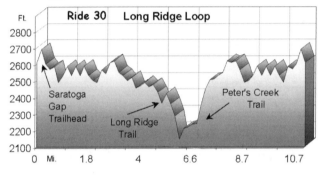

Directions/Access: See Direction/Access on Ride 29.

Bombing the Long Ridge Loop.

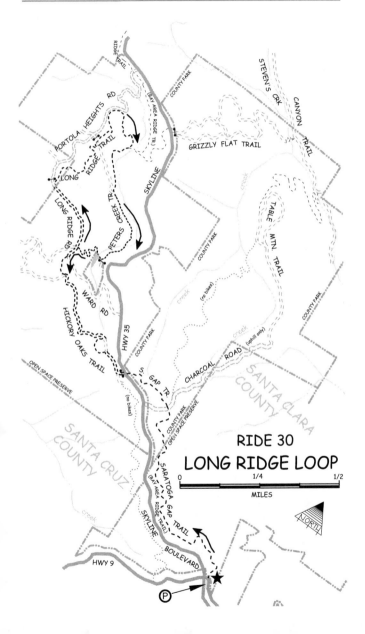

RIDE 30
LONG RIDGE LOOP

Mileage Guide	
0.0	Start riding up from the Saratoga Gap Trailhead.
1.8	At the intersection with Charcoal Road, veer left onto the singletrack.
2.2	Cross Skyline Blvd and continue on the Hickory Oaks Trail, which soon becomes a fire road.
2.4	Go left on the trail at the split. Just ahead are mind blowing views of the kind that could inspire poetry!
2.7	At the fire road, go left.
3.3	At the split with Ward Road, veer right onto the trail.
3.5	Soon you will merge straight onto the dirt road.
3.6	Intersection of Ward Road, Peter's Creek Trail, and Long Ridge Road. Go straight on Long Ridge Road.
4.1	At the gate, go right on some sweeeet singletrack!
4.9	Ignoring the road on the right, keep going straight.
5.6	After a rather steep downhill section, you reach Peters Creek Trail. Keep going straight here. (To extend this ride, go left. Options include riding the Ridge Trail, or making a far more strenuous loop with Grizzly Flat Trail (road), Canyon Trail, Table Mountain Trail, and Charcoal Road. See map.)
6.0	Stay on the trail as you pass a road up to the right.
6.7	The trail will curve around to the right and cross over a small bridge. Soon you will encounter a series of uphill switchbacks.
7.1	Back at the intersection with Long Ridge Road. Go left. The rest of the ride is an out and back.
7.2	Merge onto the trail.
7.4	Head left onto the dirt road.
8.0	Veer right onto the trail.
8.3	Go right on the short section of dirt road.
8.5	Cross Skyline Blvd and continue on the trail.
8.9	At the intersection, go straight onto the singletrack.
10.7	End of the line at the trailhead.

Access Trails & Bike Paths

*A rest spot on the West Cliff Path with a
natural bridge in the background.*

Santa Cruz has many bike paths and trails around town.
Fortunately, bikers have the option to utilize these paths to
access various mountain bike rides from town. The popular
routes are described below.

West Cliff Path

Location: West Cliff Drive in Santa Cruz.
Distance: 2.7 miles one-way.
Elevation: 15/35 ft.
Trail Surface: 100% paved path.
Terrain: West Cliff Drive; ocean; cliffs; surf.
Technical Level: Easy.
Exertion Level: Mild.

Highlights: Winding along the ocean cliffs from Cowell

Beach to Natural Bridges State Park, this is simply the most popular bike path in Santa Cruz County. Surfers, sea lions, inline skaters, whales, hippies, crashing waves, natural bridges, sunsets, a historic lighthouse and a surfing museum …this is where the action is.

Options: West Cliff is an excellent family ride in and of itself. This can also be connected with the Wilder Ranch Bike Path (Ride 32) and the San Lorenzo Riverway (Ride 34) for longer rides.

Note: There may be lots and lots and lots of people!

Directions/Access: Take Highway 1 (Mission St) north through town. Go left on Bay Street and continue until it ends at West Cliff Drive. The east end of the West Cliff Path is just above Cowell Beach and begins at the junction of Bay Street and West Cliff Drive. It follows the beach cliffs to Natural Bridges State Beach.

Looking across Cowell Beach surf break at the wharf and the Beach Boardwalk from West Cliff Path.

Wilder Ranch Bike Path

Location: Between Santa Cruz and Wilder Ranch.
Distance: 1.4 miles one-way.
Elevation: 40/90 ft.
Trail Surface: 100% paved path.
Terrain: Parallels the coastal side of Highway 1 far enough away from the noise of speeding traffic.
Technical Level: Easy.
Exertion Level: Mild.

Highlights: This paved access trail, part of the "County Bike Path," is an ideal way to get to Wilder Ranch from town or from the West Cliff Path, and makes a nice, easy, and safe family ride.

Options: Combine with Wilder Ranch/UCSC loop rides.

Note: Heavily utilized path on weekends!

Directions/Access: From Santa Cruz, take Highway 1 North (Mission St). Just as you are getting out of town, turn left on Shaffer Road (just past Western Dr) and park on the side of the road. (The bike path starts on the righthand side).

Wilder Ranch Bike Path stretches from Wilder Ranch nearly to West Cliff Path.

Arroyo Seco Canyon Path

Location: North end of Santa Cruz, off Grand View St.
Distance: 1.1 miles one-way.
Elevation: 70/260 ft.
Trail Surface: 19% singletrack; 45% fire road; 36% paved path.
Terrain: Shady canyon; eucalyptus trees; creek.
Technical Level: Easy.
Exertion Level: Moderate; somewhat steep in parts.

Highlights: While it's a short trail, Arroyo Seco is a pretty canyon filled with eucalyptus and sometimes flowing water. The trail varies from singletrack to dirt and paved bike path. This is an excellent and uncrowded way to ride to UCSC from town.

Options: The trail can be connected to West Cliff Path, Wilder Ranch Bike Path, and UCSC Bike Paths. See Ride 9.

Note: Look out for both blackberry bushes and poison oak.

Directions/Access: For the southern access; follow Highway 1 (Mission St) north through town. Turn right on Swift St and veer left onto Grand View St. After the first stop sign, there is a small park with a playground a couple hundred feet up on the right. Spot the trail between a stucco wall and a chain link fence to the right of the park. The north end of the trail is off of Meder St in the University Terrace Park.

San Lorenzo Riverway

Location: Downtown Santa Cruz.
Elevation: 0/25 ft.
Distance: 3.9 miles total.
Trail Surface: 100% paved path.
Terrain: San Lorenzo River; downtown; boardwalk.
Technical Level: Easy.
Exertion Level: Mild.

Highlights: The San Lorenzo Riverway is the safest and most scenic way to bike through the city of Santa Cruz. It provides quick access between the beach areas and downtown.

Options: These bike paths can be combined with the other paths (Rides 31-33) to access the Wilder Ranch and UCSC trails.

Note: The path is not completely continuous; there are a couple places where you will need to cross a street.

Directions/Access: The bike path extends along both banks of the San Lorenzo River from Highway 1 to the Beach Boardwalk. Access is attainable virtually anywhere along the path. The inland-side paths are off Felker St (off of Ocean St) and the shopping center off River Street/Highway 1. Beach access is from the trestle off of East Cliff Dr or the east end of the Beach Boardwalk.

Other Paths and Trails

Branciforte Creek Corridor Path

Following Branciforte Creek, this bike path can be used to access the downtown area bike paths with DeLaveaga Park. The south end of the path starts on Maye Ave off of Soquel Ave, about a block from San Lorenzo Riverway. It ends, after almost a mile, at Market St, a block from Highway 1.

Bay Street Bike Path

Surrounded by trees, a creek, and small pools, this path is actually located between the two sides of Bay St. It extends from Escalona Dr to Nobel Dr for about a mile, just before UCSC. Without a doubt, it is a safer and more pleasurable alternative than riding up Bay St to UCSC.

UCSC Bike Paths

UCSC has divided bike paths that bisect the sunny meadows of the lower campus. Each side is approximately 1 mile long. The well-marked paths start at the first intersection off of Coolidge Dr (the continuation of Bay St) near the "farm area." Heading northwest, the bike paths end at the Music Center off Meyer St. To continue onto the North Campus trails, take Meyer St to Heller St, and go north.

Arana Gulch Trail

While this trail is only a half-mile long, it cuts from the upper Santa Cruz Harbor almost all the way to Soquel Ave. This quick access to the beach areas follows Arana Creek, through open meadows and oak woodland. The north entrance is located off Agnes St, which is off of Park Way on Soquel Ave (just west of Capitola Rd).

New Brighton Trails

New Brighton State Beach includes a couple miles of minor trails in the open meadow areas. This is certainly not a biking destination, but some people ride around the area. From Park

Ave Exit off Highway 1, go toward the beach. Turn left on McGregor Drive and right on New Brighton Road. Spot the trails by the gate on the left.

Wetlands of Watsonville Paths

The Watsonville slough contains four miles of paved trails and 23 trail entrances in Watsonville neighborhoods for biking and jogging. The nature center is located at 30 Harkins Slough Rd, off of Ohlone Parkway.

Roaring Camp's Bear Mountain Trails

Roaring Camp, near Henry Cowell State Park, offers guided beginner and intermediate bike adventure tours. See www.roaringcamp.com for details.

Proposed Trails

Coast Dairies

The Coast Dairies Property, which has recently become public land, is located north of Wilder Ranch and contains 7,000 acres wonderfully scenic and diverse terrain. California State Parks is managing the coastal side of Hwy 1, while the inland portion of the property is currently being transferred to BLM management. The potential for world-class mountain biking trails is immense. Mountain Bikers of Santa Cruz, (mbosc.org) is actively participating in the implementation of the Coast Dairies Management Plan and future development of a trail system.

Monterey Bay Sanctuary Scenic Trail & Coastal Rail Trail

The MBSST will be a multi-use bicycle and pedestrian path stretching all the way from Davenport in north Santa Cruz to Lovers Point in Monterey. This is a much anticipated project which will provide continual access along the Santa Cruz coast by integrating existing bike paths and utilizing the Santa Cruz Branch Rail right of way. SCCRTC.org has more information.

Bike Jumps

Naturally high.

Aptos Jump Park (Aptos Post Office Jumps)

One of the most famous dirt jumping spots in America, the Aptos Jump Park is a home base for some of the most accomplished mountain bikers in the world, such as Cameron McCaul, Jamie Goldman, and Greg Watts. The county of Santa Cruz Parks manages the area, and allows for periodic contests such as the "Post Office Jump Jam." Please note that this park is expert-level and not for beginners.

To get here: From Santa Cruz, take Highway 1 south to State Park Dr. exit (# 435) in Aptos. Go inland (left) and take a right onto Soquel Drive. After you enter the Aptos Village area, make a left on Trout Gulch Road and left again on Cathedral Dr. The jumps are on the left. For alternate parking, see ride 19.

Bicycle Trip Bike Park

Thanks to Bicycle Trip and City of Santa Cruz, there is a cool bike park located downtown, near the Santa Cruz Wharf. The

Aptos Post Office Jumps

park features 2 and 4 foot jumps with a bowed 8 foot high wall ride. It's open 9 am to sunset daily. Its located at 35 Pacific Avenue across the street from the entrance to the Santa Cruz Municipal Wharf.

More Jumps

Dirt jumps are scattered about Santa Cruz, but are often on private land. There are unsanctioned expert-level jumps located near New Brighton State Beach along the railroad tracks off of Park Avenue across from Cabrillo Street.

Other small, unmaintained, neighborhood-style jumps are located near Brommer Park. From Hwy 1, take 41st Ave

toward the ocean a few miles. Turn right on Brommer St, after 3 stop signs the jumps are on your left, near the corner of 30th Ave and Brommer St.

Scenic dirt jumps.

Camping

New Brighton State Beach
Located 4 miles south of Santa Cruz, New Brighton State Beach features picnic areas, swimming, fishing, a nearby oak and pine forest, and developed campsites. Best of all, it is located just 1 mile from great mountain biking at the Forest of Nisene Marks. Reservations are highly recommended, especially during the summer. The beach can be reached by taking the New Brighton/Park Avenue exit off Highway 1. 831.464.6330

Seacliff State Beach
Seacliff State Beach has trailer/motorhome sites only, and is about 5 miles south of Santa Cruz. The beach is known for its fishing pier, cement ship, and a popular swimming spot. It has a covered picnic facility and an interpretive center as well. It also is a short ride to the trails of the Forest of Nisene Marks. Take the State Park Dr exit from Highway 1 in Aptos. Reservations are recommended! 831.429.2850

Manresa State Beach
About 12 miles south of Santa Cruz, Manresa State Beach features a beautiful expanse of sea and sand, with great fishing and surfing. Containing 64 tent-camping sites, RV's are not permitted. From Highway 1, south of Aptos, San Andreas Road heads southwest and continues for a few miles to Manresa, the first beach access upon reaching the coast. 831.761.1795/831.429.2850

Santa Cruz KOA (Kampgrounds-of-America)
This privately owned campground is for RV's, tents, and also has cabins. Near Manresa State Beach on San Andreas Road, the KOA has a heated pool, hot tub, mini-golf and bike rentals. 831.722.0551

Sunset State Beach
Sunset State Beach has developed campsites with pine trees,

agricultural fields, sand dunes, and ocean side picnic spots. The beach is 16 miles south of Santa Cruz via Highway 1 and San Andreas Road. Reservations are recommended in summer! 831.763.7062

The Forest of Nisene Marks State Park
Tent camping, picnic tables and barbecue pits are available for walk-in, or bike-in tent camping only. The trail camp is located six miles from the nearest parking lot. Call for a camping permit. 831.763.7062

Castle Rock State Park
Located north of Big Basin near Saratoga Gap, Castle Rock State Park's campground is on Highway 35 (Skyline Blvd), just 2 1/2 miles southeast of the junction with Highway 9. While mountain biking is not allowed, the park is known for hiking and rock climbing. 408.867.2952

Big Basin State Park
Along with good mountain biking, Big Basin has fully developed campsites nestled in the redwoods. The park is 25 miles northwest of Santa Cruz via Highway 9. In Boulder Creek turn left on Highway 236 for about 9 miles. There are also walk-in/bike-in camps along the Skyline to Sea Trail near Waddell Creek. The parking for this area is about 12 miles north of Santa Cruz on Highway 1. 831.338.8860

Henry Cowell Redwoods State Park
At Henry Cowell, you can jump on the mountain bike trails directly from your campsite, which link to Pogonip, UCSC, and Wilder Ranch. There are 113 developed campsites with $1 bike-in camping. Make reservations on the weekends and during prime summer months. The campground is closed in the winter. From Santa Cruz, take Graham Hill Road (off Ocean 831.438.2396Street) about 4 miles; the campground is on the left.

Resources

IMBA (International Mountain Biking Association)
www.imba.com
National mountain biking advocacy organization.

MBOSC (Mountain Bikers of Santa Cruz)
www.mbosc.org
The Santa Cruz mountain bike and advocacy group.

ROMP (Responsibly Organized Mountain Peddlers)
www.romp.org
Mountain cycling advocacy and events in southwest Bay Area.

Team Wrong Way
www.teamwrongway.com
Bay Area racing organization.

Trailworkers.com
www.trailworkers.com
Santa Cruz county trail work organization.

Santa Cruz County Visitor Center & Information
www.santacruzca.org
1211 Ocean St. Santa Cruz, CA
800.833.3494 / 831.425.1234

Santa Cruz Parks & Recreation
www.santacruzparksandrec.com
831.420.5270

Santa Cruz State Parks
www.SantaCruzStateParks.org

California State Parks
www.parks.ca.gov

Mountain Bike Events

Breathe deep here.

Sea Otter Classic; Monterey
www.seaotterclassic.com
One of the biggest mountain bike events in the West; April.

Jump Jam; Aptos/Santa Cruz
www.jumpjam.net
Dirt Jump events at Aptos Jump Park and Bicycle Trip Bike Park.

Central Coast Race Series; Central Coast
www.cccx.org
Cross country, downhill, and cyclo-cross races.

Surf City Cyclocross; Soquel/Santa Cruz
surfcitycx.blogspot.com/
Local NCNCA sanctioned Cyclocross races.

Peak Season Cyclocross; Santa Cruz
www.cyclocross.cx
Year-round local cyclocross races.

24-Hours of Adrenalin; Monterey
www.24hoursofadrenalin.com
NORBA sanctioned events in spring/summer.

Take a Kid Mountain Biking Day (MBOSC); Santa Cruz
www.mbosc.org
Introduces mountain biking to kids.

Carrot Fest at Wilder Ranch (MBOSC); Santa Cruz
www.mbosc.org
Improving relations between mountain bikers and equestrians.

For up-to-date information on local events and races, see
www.mbosc.org, www.wrongway.com, www.csmevents.com,
and/or www.ncnca.org/mtb**.**

Saratoga gap on a clear Spring day.

Bike Shops

Even better than it looks.

Another Bike Shop
2361 Mission St; Santa Cruz; 831.427.2232

The Bicycle Trip
1127 Soquel Ave; Santa Cruz; 831.427.2580

Sprockets
1420 Mission St; Santa Cruz; 831.426.7623

The Bicycle Shop Santa Cruz
1325 Mission St; Santa Cruz; 831.454.0909

Armadillo Cyclery
1211 Mission St; Santa Cruz; 831.426.7299

Bike Co-op
1156 High St; Santa Cruz; 831.457.8281

Spokesman Bicycles
231 Cathcart St; Santa Cruz; 831.423.6062

Dave's Custom Bikes
318 Pacific Ave; Santa Cruz; 831.423.8923

Bill's Bike Repair
2628 Soquel Ave; Santa Cruz; 831.477.0511

Bike Doctor
2917 Granite Creek Rd, Scotts Valley; 408.202.8833

Recycled Bikes of Santa Cruz
2420 7th Ave; Santa Cruz; 831.465.9955

The Bike Church
224 Walnut Ave, Santa Cruz; 831.425.2453

Family Cycling Center
914 41st Ave; Capitola; 831.475.3883

Amsterdam Bicycles and Coffee Shop
2-1231 E. Cliff Dr; Capitola; 831.475.1394

The Bike Station of Aptos
8061 Aptos St., Aptos; 831.688.4169

Scotts Valley Cycle Sport
245-J Mount Hermon Rd; Scotts Valley; 831.440.9070

T N L Bikes
1916 Freedom Blvd, Freedom; 831.722.1233

Watsonville Cyclery
1202 Freedom Blvd, Watsonville; 831.724.1646

*Keeping up
with the
ocean
breezes.*

Index of Rides By Category

Ride 19   Aptos Creek Fire Road with Ride 20 addition
Ride 21   Hinckley Basin Fire Road with Ride 20 addition
Ride 24   Inner Demo Loop (double loop)
Ride 5   Wilder-Gray Whale Loop
Ride 9   Arroyo Seco-UCSC-Wilder Loop

Insane Downhills

(includes uphill pedaling as well)
Ride 15   Top of the World Loop
Ride 24   Inner Demo Loop
Ride 19   Aptos Creek Fire Road
Ride 27   Big Basin Loop
Ride 28A   Gazos Creek Road (one way shuttle)
Ride 2   Wilder Ridge Loop
Ride 5   Wilder-Gray Whale Loop

Expedition Big-Day Rides

Ride 22   Epic Nisene-Demo Ride
Ride 13   Redwoods to Coast Ride (loop option)
Ride 27   Big Basin Loop (with spur trail exploration)

Multi Interest Rides

Rides 1-6   All Wilder Ranch Rides; (Cultural Preserve)
Ride 5   Wilder Gray Whale Loop; (lime kiln, quarry)
Ride 1   Old Cove/Ohlone Bluff Trail;
            (natural bridges & marine life)
Ride 26   Waddell Creek/Skyline to Sea Trail;
            (hike to waterfall)
Ride 27   Big Basin Loop;
            (redwoods, ocean and mountain views)
Ride 12   Henry Cowell Loop; (observation tower, San
            Lorenzo River, redwoods)
Ride 15   Top of the World Loop; (disc golf)
Ride 30   Long Ridge Loop; (panoramic ocean & mountain
            views; rock climbing in the area)
Ride 19   Aptos Creek Fire Road; (Loma Prieta Earthquake

Center; hikes to waterfalls, logging & mill sites).

Quick Fixes
Ride 18   Vienna Woods Combo Loop
Ride 17   Aptos Rancho Trail
Ride 15   Top of the World Loop
Ride 16   Figure 8 Loop
Ride 11   U-Con Trail
Ride 29   Saratoga Gap Trail
Ride 21   Hinckley Basin Fire Road

Multi-Park/ Interregional Rides
Ride 22   Ultra Mega Nisene-Demo Ride
Ride 9   Arroyo Seco-UCSC-Wilder Loop
Ride 8   Cowell-Wilder Regional Trail
Ride 13   Redwoods to Coast Ride
Ride 30   Long Ridge Loop

Santa Cruz Classics
Ride 2   Wilder Ridge Loop
Ride 4   Wilder Singletrack Loop
Ride 15   Top of the World Loop with Figure 8 Loop
Ride 1   Old Cove Landing/Ohlone Bluff Trail
Ride 23   Outer Demo Loop (or Inner Demo Loop)
Ride 19   Aptos Creek Fire Road
Ride 26   Waddel Creek/Skyline to the Sea Trail

*Singletrack
Mind.*

Index of Maps

Riding Santa Cruz Style.

Another day in paradise.

Index of Trails and Rides

Photos are located on page numbers in bold, while maps are in italicized pages below:

Special Thanks

Thanks to all our friends and family that helped with creating this book! Big loud Thank You's go out to Jay and Kira Brown, Allison Bell, Jon Diller, and Jeff Block for helping with the rides and pictures! Jay, thanks sooo much for all the posing (don't worry, you're not a poser).

We appreciate the editing help from the Blocks and the endless support from all the Dillers. We are also grateful for help from Randall Cornish and John Moynier. Special thanks to Rob Roskopp and Santa Cruz Bicycles for providing the insane bikes!

The Authors

Dave grew up exploring the forests in Santa Cruz. In 1983, he started mountain biking the Forest of Nisene Marks and other Santa Cruz areas. In addition to biking, he loves whitewater kayaking, kitesurfing, snowboarding, and basically anything outdoors. Dave went to Soquel High School and graduated from the University of California Santa Cruz.

Allison Diller learned to mountain bike in Santa Cruz and has been passionate about the sport ever since. When not riding, she loves playing beach volleyball, kiteboarding, and adventuring around with husband Dave. She graduated from Harbor High School and University of California Santa Barbara.

Dave and Allison love mountain biking anywhere there is great singletrack, taking photographs, making maps, and hanging outside in nature. They wrote this book to share their passion!

Book Information

See *extremeline.com* for more information on books. Check out The Mud Blog, *blog.extremeline.com*, for trail updates. If you have any questions, suggestions, or comments, please email them to *books@extremeline.com*.

Extremeline Mountain Bike Guides also available:

Mountain Biking Mammoth (ISBN-13 978-0-9723361-1-6)
Mountain Biking San Diego (ISBN-13 978-0-9723361-3-0)

What more can be said?